Mr. Boston Cordial Cooking Guide

MR. BOSTON CORDIAL COOKING GUIDE

 WARNER BOOKS

A Warner Communications Company

Recipes developed and tested under the supervision of the International Institute of Foods and Family Living, Inc., Chicago, Illinois.

Warner Books, Inc., 75 Rockefeller Plaza, New York, NY 10019

Ⓦ A Warner Communications Company

Printed in the United States of America

First printing: November 1982
10 9 8 7 6 5 4 3 2 1

Book design: H. Roberts Design

Library of Congress Cataloging in Publication Data

Mr. Boston cordial cooking guide.

    Includes index.
    1. Cookery (Liquors)   I. Title: Mister Boston cordial cooking guide.

TX726.M7	641.6′25	82-2652
ISBN 0-446-51252-4		AACR2

TABLE OF CONTENTS

Introduction

Welcome! Your Mr. Boston Cordial Cooking Guide introduces you to the joy of spirits as an ingredient in cooking. Whether you are an eager novice, an accomplished host or hostess, or even a professional gourmet, here is an opportunity to explore the spirited approach to every course from appetizer to entree to dessert and beverage. Interesting new dishes and old stand-by favorites are made different and better—more sparkling and animated in flavor. Spirits may spark a marinade or basting juice, add a gentle accent to a casserole, or enliven a sauce. In every case, they impart an elegance and subtlety that is distinctive.

Perhaps you have already begun this kind of invention on your own—adding sherry to your soup, brandy to a sauce, or a dash of applejack to a fresh fruit salad. You may feel that you have entered an uncharted territory without a map, for there are no general guidelines for cooking with cordials as there are for selecting wines—white and dry with fish, red with meat. When master chefs add a splash of this or a dash of that fine spirit to a dish, they use both instinct and experience in choosing the bottle and determining how long to let the liquid flow. You may still wonder how much you can add to create an accent without overwhelming. This book can give you some of their expertise.

Begin by following each recipe to the letter as a guarantee of superior results. Then, as you gain confidence, develop your own variations.

The Liquor Index, pages 134–136, arranges the recipes according to the spirit(s) used in each. What dishes are enriched by apricot-flavored brandy? Where does gin add piquancy? If you love the taste of crème de menthe, what entrée profits by its addition?

And what about serving an entire meal of foods in which spirits serve as flavor accents? How can you decide what conflicts, what contrasts and complements? The Menu Guide, page 127, gives you the elements for planning meals, whether simple or formal, with variety: hot with cold, bright against dark, a range of sweet to tart.

Whether you first try this book by checking your liquor cabinet and finding a recipe to fit, or by choosing a dish that intrigues you—perhaps one that uses a cordial or liqueur you have never before used—prepare yourself for a new adventure in taste. Mr. Boston Cordial Cooking Guide can add a new artistry to your cooking and a fresh dimension to your dining, while enhancing your reputation as a marvelous host or hostess.

Appetizers/Soups

Spirits transform the appetizer or soup course from a simple introduction to the meal to an intriguing invitation to a feast. Used as snacks, spirited appetizers become memorable accompaniments to drinks at a cocktail party.

In this chapter seafood, the flavor enhanced by such varied spirits as Mandarine Napoleon and cream sherry, is served in hot canapés or cold in frosted cocktail glasses.

Sweet and Sour Sausage Balls derive their accent not from minced ginger root but from ginger brandy.

Borscht is transformed from a hearty peasant dish into fare fit for a czar with the addition of vodka, and the natural goodness of delicious fruit is made sumptuous with apple-flavored brandy in Veal-Stuffed Apples.

The dishes described here also may be amplified into elegant lunches, brunches, or after-theater main courses when you serve them with bread and salad.

SEAFOOD TOAST

Blend crab, shrimp, Mandarine Napoleon, egg, onion, cornstarch, salt, and hot pepper sauce. Spread mixture on bread slices and coat with bread crumbs, pressing crumbs into surface; chill 15 minutes. Cut each slice into four triangles. Heat oil in skillet; fry triangles, spread side down, until golden brown. Turn and brown other side.

40 appetizers

1 six-ounce can crabmeat
1 six-ounce can shrimp
¼ cup Mandarine Napoleon
1 egg, beaten
2 tablespoons minced onion
1 tablespoon cornstarch
1 teaspoon salt
⅛ teaspoon hot pepper sauce
10 slices stale bread, crusts trimmed
Fine, dry bread crumbs
1 cup oil

COGNAC STEAMED MUSSELS

Combine onion, garlic, cognac, lemon juice, parsley, basil, and mustard seed in a saucepan; bring to a boil, reduce heat, and simmer 5–10 minutes or until onions are soft. Add mussels, cover, and simmer 7–10 minutes until all the mussels open. Remove mussels to serving dish. Add cream to pan juices and cook over medium heat 2–3 minutes. Season to taste with salt and pepper. Pour sauce over mussels and serve.

4 servings

1 cup thinly sliced onion
2 cloves garlic, minced
½ cup Rémy Martin V.S.O.P. Cognac
2 tablespoons lemon juice
¼ cup chopped parsley
¾ teaspoon basil
½ teaspoon crushed mustard seed
2 pounds raw mussels
½ cup heavy cream
Salt
White pepper

5

CHILLED STUFFED MUSSELS

¼ cup Amaretto di
  Saronno
2 tablespoons currants
1 tablespoon minced
  shallots
1 tablespoon butter
¾–1 cup cooked rice
1 tablespoon tomato
  paste
2 teaspoons lemon juice
⅛ teaspoon dried lemon
  peel
⅛ teaspoon ground
  cloves
Dash cayenne pepper
1 pound steamed
  mussels

Combine Amaretto di Saronno and currants in saucepan. Bring to a boil; reduce heat and simmer 2–3 minutes. Remove from heat and let stand 30 minutes. Sauté shallots in butter 3–4 minutes. Remove from heat and add currants and liquid, rice, tomato paste, lemon juice and peel, and seasonings; mix well. Separate mussel shells and detach mussel. Place mussel in half the shell, discarding other half. Top each mussel with about 1 tablespoon stuffing mixture. Cover and chill until ready to serve.

12–15 appetizers

BROILED STUFFED OYSTERS

½ cup chopped parsley
⅓ cup minced shallots
2 cloves garlic, minced
¼ cup butter
¼ cup Mr. Boston
  Anisette
½ cup seasoned, dry
  bread crumbs
Black pepper
24 oysters in shell
24 small pieces raw
  bacon, about 1½
  inches square

Sauté parsley, shallots, and garlic in butter over low heat 2–3 minutes. Add anisette, increase heat, and cook 2–3 minutes until most of the liquid has evaporated. Add bread crumbs and cook 1 minute more, stirring constantly. Season with pepper and set aside. Open oysters, discarding half the shell. Place oysters in remaining half shell on baking sheet. Cover each oyster with scant tablespoon of stuffing; top with 1 piece of bacon. Broil until bacon crisps and stuffing browns. Serve immediately.

24 appetizers

SEAFRUIT STUFFED MUSHROOMS

Remove stems from mushrooms and chop enough of them to make ¼ cup. Sauté chopped mushroom stems, celery, shallots, and garlic in butter until lightly browned. Add scallops, clams, bread crumbs, ¾ cup sherry, Parmesan cheese, ¼ cup Swiss cheese, and seasonings. Cook 3–5 minutes, stirring constantly. Fill mushroom caps with mixture and place in baking pan. Pour remaining ¼ cup sherry over mushrooms and sprinkle with remaining ¼ cup Swiss cheese. Bake in preheated 325°F. oven 12–15 minutes.

24 appetizers

24 large mushrooms, cleaned
¼ cup chopped celery
1 tablespoon chopped shallots
2 cloves garlic, minced
½ cup butter
¼ pound chopped scallops
1 six-and-a-half-ounce can minced clams, drained
1 cup fine, dry bread crumbs
1 cup Balfour Cream Sherry
⅓ cup grated Parmesan cheese
½ cup shredded Swiss cheese
2 tablespoons chopped parsley
½ teaspoon salt
½ teaspoon sage
½ teaspoon thyme
¼ teaspoon pepper

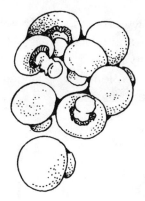

꿀꿀꿀꿀꿀

SUNNY SCALLOP SURPRISE

⅔ cup lime juice
3 tablespoons oil
3 tablespoons Glenmore
  Gin
2 green onions, sliced
2 cloves garlic, minced
1 teaspoon salt
½ teaspoon coriander
4–6 drops hot pepper
  sauce
1 pound bay scallops

Combine lime juice, oil, gin, onions, garlic, and seasonings in mixing bowl; blend thoroughly. Stir in scallops. Cover and refrigerate 6–8 hours before serving. Serve in frosted cocktail glasses or coquille shells.

4–6 servings

꿀꿀꿀꿀꿀

CUCUMBER SEAFOOD DUNK

1 cup sour cream
1½ cups chopped
  cucumber
2 tablespoons
  Glenmore Vodka
2 tablespoons lemon
  juice
2 tablespoons chopped
  parsley
1 teaspoon tarragon
  vinegar
1 teaspoon tarragon
1 teaspoon salt
¼ teaspoon white
  pepper
¼ teaspoon celery salt
½ cup heavy cream,
  whipped

Place sour cream and cucumber in blender or food processor and process until cucumber is finely minced, 00–40 seconds. Stir in vodka, lemon juice, parsley, vinegar, and seasonings. Fold cucumber mixture into whipped cream. Refrigerate at least 30 minutes before serving. Serve with crab legs or cold poached salmon

Makes 3 cups

BROILED CHICKEN DRUMETTES

Cut wings into 2 sections; place in baking pan. Combine remaining ingredients in saucepan and bring to boil. Boil 5 minutes. Pour sauce over chicken wings and marinate at least 2 hours. (For best results, marinate overnight.) Place chicken wings in the broiler 4 inches from heat and broil 8–10 minutes on each side, brushing twice with reserved marinade.

10–12 servings

3 pounds chicken wings
½ cup Mr. Boston Triple Sec
6 tablespoons frozen concentrated orange juice
3 tablespoons chili sauce
2 tablespoons honey
2 tablespoons soy sauce
2 tablespoons vegetable oil
¼ teaspoon dry mustard
1 clove garlic, minced

SPICY BABY RIBS

Combine Triple Sec, soy sauce, garlic, and spices. Pour over baby back ribs and marinate at least 2 hours. (For best results marinate overnight.) Place ribs on a rack in a roasting pan. Bake in preheated 325°F. oven for 1 hour, basting frequently with marinade. Increase heat to 400°F. and bake another 25 minutes.

6 servings

¼ cup Mr. Boston Triple Sec
¼ cup soy sauce
2 cloves garlic, minced
¼ teaspoon cinnamon
¼ teaspoon ground cloves
¼ teaspoon ground anise
¼ teaspoon ground fennel
Dash cayenne pepper
2 pounds baby back ribs

FISH BITES

2 eggs
1 cup cold water
¾ cup flour
1 tablespoon cornstarch
½ teaspoon baking
  powder
½ teaspoon salt
1½–2 pounds fillet of sole
  or flounder, cut into
  julienne strips
Oil
Cream Sherry Sauce or
  Anisette Mayonnaise
  (see below)

Beat together eggs, water, flour, cornstarch, baking powder, and salt until smooth. Dip fish pieces in batter and fry in 1 inch hot oil until golden brown. Drain. Serve hot with Cream Sherry Sauce or Anisette Mayonnaise.

8 servings

Cream Sherry Sauce

½ cup butter
2 egg yolks
2 tablespoons lemon
  juice
2 tablespoons Balfour
  Cream Sherry
2 teaspoons Dijon
  mustard
¼ teaspoon salt
Dash cayenne pepper

Heat butter until bubbly. Place egg yolks, lemon juice, sherry, mustard, salt, and pepper in blender jar and blend until smooth, 5–10 seconds. Gradually add butter while blending and process until smooth, 10–15 seconds.

Broiled Chicken Drumettes; Fish Bites with Cream Sherry Sauce
Sherried Fish Chowder and Senegalese Soup

Anisette Mayonnaise

Combine yolks, mustard, pepper, salt, and lemon juice in medium-sized bowl. Beating with whisk, add ½ cup oil drop by drop. Add remaining oil in a steady stream, beating continuously. Gradually add anisette. Cover and refrigerate until ready to use.

2 egg yolks
½ teaspoon Dijon mustard
Dash cayenne pepper
½ teaspoon salt
1 tablespoon lemon juice
1 cup olive oil
⅓ cup Mr. Boston Anisette

SWEET AND SOUR SAUSAGE BALLS

Combine sausage, egg, and bread crumbs; shape mixture into ¾-inch balls. Cook in hot oil until brown on all sides; drain. Combine remaining ingredients in saucepan and bring to a boil. Reduce heat, add sausage balls, and simmer 30 minutes.

6–8 servings

1 pound bulk pork sausage
1 egg, beaten
¾ cup soft bread crumbs
1 tablespoon oil
1 fifteen-ounce can condensed tomato soup
¼ cup Mr. Boston Triple Sec
¼ cup Mr. Boston Ginger-Flavored Brandy
2 tablespoons brown sugar
1 tablespoon Dijon mustard
1 tablespoon soy sauce
2 teaspoons vinegar
¼ teaspoon ginger
1 clove garlic, minced

MR. BOSTON CORDIAL COOKING GUIDE

CHICKEN LIVER PÂTÉ

1 pound chicken livers, cleaned
6 tablespoons butter
⅓ cup finely chopped onions
1 clove garlic, minced
⅓ cup plus 1 tablespoon Mr. Boston Apple-Flavored Brandy
1 teaspoon paprika
1 teaspoon lemon juice
½ teaspoon salt
⅛ teaspoon white pepper

Sauté livers in 2 tablespoons butter over medium-high heat until livers are brown on outside but still pink on the inside. Remove and reserve. Melt 2 tablespoons butter over low heat. Add onions and garlic; cook 3–4 minutes. Add ⅓ cup brandy and paprika. Increase heat and cook 4–5 minutes or until liquid is reduced by half. Add livers to mixture and cool. Place mixture in blender or food processor. Add remaining butter, 1 tablespoon brandy, lemon juice, salt, and pepper and blend until smooth. Chill several hours or overnight before serving.

10–12 servings

VEGETABLE TERRINE

Carrot Layer

2½ cups coarsely chopped carrots, cooked
1 tablespoon butter
¼ cup heavy cream
2 eggs
2 tablespoons fine, dry bread crumbs
½ teaspoon salt
⅛ teaspoon pepper
⅛ teaspoon nutmeg

Combine carrots, butter, and cream in saucepan; cook until liquid has evaporated. Place in blender jar or food processor with eggs and blend until smooth. Stir in bread crumbs and seasonings. Set aside.

12

Green Bean Layer

Combine bean purée, eggs, bread crumbs, cream, anisette, and seasonings; beat until smooth. Set aside.

2½ cups cut green beans, cooked, drained, and puréed
2 eggs
¼ cup fine, dry bread crumbs
2 tablespoons heavy cream
1 tablespoon Mr. Boston Anisette
¼ teaspoon tarragon
½ teaspoon salt
⅛ teaspoon pepper

Mushroom Layer

Sauté onions and garlic in butter 2–3 minutes; add mushrooms and cook until tender. Stir in sherry and cook until liquid has evaporated. Remove from heat; stir in egg, bread crumbs, and seasonings.

To assemble terrine, butter and line with wax paper bottom and sides of 9 × 5-inch glass loaf pan. Evenly spread carrot mixture in bottom of pan. Evenly spread bean mixture over carrots and repeat with mushroom mixture. Top with piece of buttered foil. Place in pan of hot water and bake in preheated 350°F. oven for 50 minutes or until puffed and set. Cool and refrigerate overnight before unmolding and serving.

1 cup finely chopped onions
1 clove garlic, minced
2 tablespoons butter
1 pound mushrooms, finely chopped
¼ cup Balfour Cream Sherry
1 egg
2 tablespoons fine, dry bread crumbs
½ teaspoon salt
⅛ teaspoon pepper
⅛ teaspoon tarragon
⅛ teaspoon nutmeg

MUSHROOMS À LA GRECQUE

1½ cups water
½ cup olive oil
½ cup Mr. Boston
  Anisette
1 cup chopped
  tomatoes
¼ cup chopped celery
2 cloves garlic, minced
2 tablespoons lemon
  juice
1 tablespoon vinegar
1 tablespoon salt
1 teaspoon fennel
1 teaspoon coriander
½ teaspoon oregano
½ teaspoon rosemary
2 bay leaves
¼ teaspoon pepper
1 pound mushrooms

Combine all ingredients except mushrooms in saucepan. Simmer 1 hour. Add mushrooms and cook 15 minutes. Cool and chill 24 hours before serving.

6 servings

ROQUEFORT-STUFFED PEARS

1 cup crumbled bleu or
  Roquefort cheese
1 three-ounce package
  cream cheese
1 tablespoon Rémy
  Martin V.S.O.P. Cognac
1 tablespoon Mr. Boston
  Cherry-Flavored
  Brandy
6–7 pears, cored

Blend cheeses, cognac, and brandy until smooth. Stuff into cored pears. Cover and refrigerate until filling is firm, 2–3 hours. Slice to serve.

12–15 servings

VEAL-STUFFED APPLES

Sauté onion and garlic in 1 tablespoon butter over low heat 3–5 minutes. Meanwhile, cut tops off apples; reserve. Core apples without going through bottom and scoop out insides, leaving ¼-inch shell intact. Finely chop scooped apple, add to onion mixture, and cook over medium-low heat 5 minutes. Add ¼ cup brandy and cook until most of the liquid has evaporated, 5–6 minutes; remove from heat. Add veal, cream, egg yolk, and seasonings.

Stuff apples with mixture, returning tops to apples. Place in 2-quart baking dish; pour remaining ¼ cup brandy and water over the apples. Cover and bake in preheated 350°F. oven 45–50 minutes or until apples are tender. Remove apples and keep warm. Cook liquid over medium heat about 10 minutes. Stir in remaining 2 tablespoons butter. Cut apples into quarters and pour sauce over apples to serve.

12–14 servings

- ¼ cup minced onion
- 1 clove garlic, minced
- 3 tablespoons butter, softened
- 6–7 large red Delicious apples
- ½ cup Mr. Boston Apple-Flavored Brandy
- ½ pound ground veal
- 2 tablespoons heavy cream
- 1 egg yolk
- ½ teaspoon salt
- ⅛ teaspoon white pepper
- ⅛ teaspoon allspice
- ¼ cup water

CHEESE FONDUE

Heat wine in fondue dish or casserole. Add garlic, bring to a boil, and boil 5 minutes. Reduce heat and add cheeses gradually, stirring constantly, until cheese is melted. Blend cornstarch with brandy and

stir into cheese mixture. Cook over medium heat until smooth and thickened. Stir in salt, pepper, and nutmeg. Serve with bread cubes or crudités.

4–6 servings

- 1½ cups Lawrence Fumé Blanc
- 1 clove garlic, minced
- 2 cups shredded Fontina cheese
- 2 cups shredded Havarti cheese
- 1 tablespoon cornstarch
- ⅓ cup Mr. Boston Cherry-Flavored Brandy
- ⅛ teaspoon salt
- ⅛ teaspoon white pepper
- ⅛ teaspoon nutmeg

꽃꽃꽃꽃꽃

TIPSY CHEESE SPREAD

8 ounces cottage cheese
4 anchovy fillets
2 tablespoons kümmel
2 tablespoons paprika
1 tablespoon caraway
  seeds
1 teaspoon dry mustard
½ teaspoon salt
½ teaspoon pepper
3 tablespoons capers
1 eight-ounce package
  cream cheese
½ cup butter
2 tablespoons Glenmore
  Gin
¼ cup chopped chives

Place cottage cheese, anchovy fillets, kümmel, paprika, caraway seeds, mustard, salt, and pepper in blender jar; blend until smooth. Add capers and blend a few seconds more. Beat in cream cheese, butter, and gin. Cover and refrigerate. Just before serving blend in chives. This spread is best when aged for 1 week before serving.

Makes 2½ cups

꽃꽃꽃꽃꽃

FESTIVE CHEESE POT

½ cup beer
3 tablespoons kümmel
¼ cup minced onions
2 tablespoons butter
1 tablespoon Dijon
  mustard
¼ teaspoon hot pepper
  sauce
¼ teaspoon salt
4 cups shredded sharp
  Cheddar cheese
½ cup cooked, crumbled
  bacon

Bring beer, kümmel, and onions to a boil. Cook over medium heat 10 minutes. Remove from heat; whisk in butter, mustard, hot pepper sauce, and salt. Stir in cheese. Place in blender or food processor and blend until smooth. Stir in bacon bits and chill overnight before serving. Serve with French bread or crackers.

6–8 servings

CREAMY LEEK AND POTATO SOUP

Sauté leeks and garlic in butter over low heat until translucent, 10–15 minutes. Add potatoes and kümmel and cook, stirring frequently, 5 minutes. Add chicken broth and simmer 30 minutes. Cool slightly and purée in food processor or blender. Return to heat and blend in half-and-half. Heat through without boiling. Season to taste with salt and pepper. Stir in chives just before serving.

6–8 servings

3 cups chopped leeks, white part only
1 clove garlic, minced
¼ cup butter
2 cups peeled, diced potatoes
¼ cup kümmel
3 cups chicken broth
1 cup half-and-half
Salt
Pepper
2 tablespoons chopped chives

IMPERIAL BORSCHT

Cook beets in boiling, salted water until tender. Remove from water with slotted spoon and drain. Peel beets, cut into julienne strips, and set aside. Add cabbage to beet water and cook 10 minutes. Sauté onion in butter over low heat until tender but not brown. Add broth to onions; bring to a boil. Add cabbage and cooking water, beets, caraway seeds, sugar, salt, and pepper; simmer 10 minutes, skimming top as needed. Add lemon juice and return to a boil. Immediately remove from heat and stir in vodka. Serve with dollop of sour cream.

6 servings

1 pound fresh beets
2 cups shredded cabbage
½ cup chopped onion
¼ cup butter
1 quart chicken broth
2 teaspoons caraway seeds
1 teaspoon sugar
1 teaspoon salt
¼ teaspoon pepper
3 tablespoons lemon juice
½ cup Glenmore Vodka
Sour cream

PIZZA SOUP

½ pound pepperoni, chopped
¼ cup chopped onions
¼ cup chopped green pepper
¼ cup chopped mushrooms
2 tablespoons butter
3 cups beef broth
1 fifteen-ounce can pizza sauce
1 cup diced tomatoes
½ cup Mr. Boston Anisette
1 tablespoon oregano
2 cloves garlic, minced
1 loaf Italian bread
1½ cups shredded Mozzarella cheese

Brown pepperoni and vegetables in butter. Add broth, pizza sauce, tomatoes, anisette, and seasonings; bring to a boil. Reduce heat and simmer 1 hour. Slice and toast Italian bread. Place 1 slice in bottom of individual ovenproof bowls. Add soup. Cover with cheese and broil until cheese bubbles and browns. Serve with a salad and you have a complete meal.

8 servings

POTAGE OF ARTICHOKE

5 cups chicken broth
2 fourteen-ounce cans artichoke hearts, drained and chopped
½ cup chopped onion
3 cloves garlic, minced
⅔ cup half-and-half
½ cup Balfour Cream Sherry
1 teaspoon chervil
Salt
Pepper

Combine chicken broth, artichokes, onion, and garlic in saucepan. Bring to a boil; reduce heat and simmer 20 minutes. Purée mixture. Stir 1 cup warm soup into cream and combine with remaining soup. Add sherry and chervil. Heat without boiling. Season to taste with salt and pepper.

8 servings

BRANDIED ONION SOUP

Cook onion in butter over low heat until golden brown, about 30 minutes. Add brandy and sugar; cook over medium-high heat 5–6 minutes. Stir in flour and seasonings. Cook, stirring constantly, 1 minute longer. Gradually add beef broth, stirring until smooth; cover and simmer 1 hour. Stir in cream and heat through before serving.

8–10 servings

12 large onions, thinly sliced
½ cup butter
¾ cup Mr. Boston Five Star Brandy
1 tablespoon sugar
2 tablespoons flour
Pinch thyme
1 bay leaf
1 teaspoon salt
¼ teaspoon pepper
2 quarts beef broth
½ cup heavy cream

FROSTY FRUIT NECTAR

Soak dried fruits in water and 1 cup brandy 30 minutes. Combine soaked fruits and liquid with sugar, apple cider, apricot brandy, apple, lemon juice and peel, and cinnamon. Bring to a boil; reduce heat and simmer 10 minutes, stirring occasionally. Blend cornstarch with 2 tablespoons water until smooth and add to soup. Bring to a boil again and cook until thickened, stirring constantly. Remove from heat, allow to cool, and chill thoroughly before serving.

6 servings

1 cup dried, chopped apricots
1 cup chopped prunes
1 cup raisins
5 cups water
1 cup Mr. Boston Five Star Brandy
1 cup sugar
2 cups apple cider
¼ cup Mr. Boston Apricot Flavored Brandy
1 apple, peeled and chopped
6 tablespoons lemon juice
1 tablespoon grated lemon peel
¼ teaspoon cinnamon
2 tablespoons cornstarch

SHERRIED FISH CHOWDER

1 quart beef broth
2 cups clam broth
2 cups water
1 cup diced carrots
1 cup diced celery
½ cup diced onions
1 cup tomato purée
2 tablespoons lemon
  juice
1 teaspoon
  Worcestershire sauce
½ teaspoon marjoram
¼ teaspoon thyme
Dash hot pepper sauce
¼ cup butter, melted
½ cup flour
½ cup Balfour Cream
  Sherry
1½ teaspoons salt
½ teaspoon pepper
2 pounds white fish
  fillets, cut into 1-inch
  pieces

Combine broths, water, vegetables, tomato puree, and seasonings; simmer 30 minutes. Blend butter and flour until smooth. Whisk butter-flour mixture into 1 cup hot soup broth; blend until smooth. Return to hot liquid. Stir in sherry, salt, and pepper; bring to a boil. Reduce heat and simmer 15 minutes. Add fish; simmer 15 minutes or until fish flakes easily. Serve hot. This hearty soup is good as a main dish.

8–10 servings

SENEGALESE SOUP

Cook vegetables in 2 tablespoons butter over medium heat until golden brown, stirring occasionally. Stir in curry powder, cinnamon sticks, bay leaves, cloves, parsley, broth, Amaretto di Saronno, tomato paste, and jelly. Bring to a boil, reduce heat, and simmer 1 hour. Blend flour with remaining, melted butter to make paste. Whisk into soup a little at a time. Cook 5–6 minutes, stirring constantly, until soup thickens. Strain and season to taste with salt and pepper. Chill. Stir in heavy cream just before serving. Sprinkle with nutmeg and toasted coconut.

6–8 servings

1 small onion, chopped
1 carrot, chopped
1 stalk celery, chopped
5 tablespoons butter
1 teaspoon curry powder
3 small cinnamon sticks
2 bay leaves
1 teaspoon whole cloves
4 sprigs parsley
4 cups chicken broth
½ cup Amaretto di Saronno
1 tablespoon tomato paste
1 tablespoon red currant jelly
3 tablespoons flour
Salt
White pepper
2 cups heavy cream
Nutmeg
Toasted flaked coconut

CREAMY RATATOUILLE SOUP

¾ cup chopped onion
1 clove garlic, minced
2 tablespoons olive oil
4 cups peeled, chopped
  eggplant
1 cup chopped green
  pepper
2 cups chopped zucchini
6 cups chicken broth
¼ cup Glenmore Gin
1 teaspoon salt
½ teaspoon oregano
¼ teaspoon white pepper
¼ teaspoon basil
½ cup heavy cream

Sauté onion and garlic in olive oil over medium heat 3 minutes. Add eggplant and green pepper and cook 5 minutes. Add zucchini; cover and cook 5 minutes. Add chicken broth, gin, and seasonings. Bring to a boil, reduce heat and simmer, uncovered, 30 minutes. Remove from heat and cool 10–15 minutes. Purée and return to saucepan. Stir in cream and heat thoroughly without boiling. Chill 3–4 hours before serving.

8 servings

Entrées

The entrée declares the character of the meal. Whether meat, fish, or fowl, it is the main course and the instance in which the spirited accent can be most definitive. In this section you will find recipes that rise to your occasions, whatever they may be. A simple sole is made intriguingly different by the addition of cognac, anisette, and pine nuts. A pot roast becomes a memorable event when it is embellished with apples and brandy. Prime ribs achieve new distinction when accompanied by Yorkshire Pudding and gravy made savory with Scotch.

These recipes also serve as a guide to the enhancement of flavor in entrées that are already part of your repertoire. Butters and sauces using cognac, whiskey, brandy, and gin provide versatile variations for dishes made from beef, fowl, or fish. Instead of the customary mint jelly accompaniment to lamb, we tell you how to make Crème de Menthe Sauce or even more exotic Coffee Brandy Cream Sauce. Instead of orange sauce for pork, we invite you to try a recipe that uses tangerine juice, peel, and Mandarine Napoleon.

You will learn how to use several spirit flavors effectively in one dish, as in Seafood with Vegetables and Whiskey, where Scotch is used as a flambéing spirit, wine as a deglazer, and cognac as an ingredient in the sauce. You will also discover the magic ingredient that transforms any fish suitable for poaching—apricot brandy.

SWORDFISH TERIYAKI

Combine water, soy sauce, brandy, onion, garlic, and ginger. Pour over fish and marinate 2 hours to overnight. Broil 2–3 minutes; brush with marinade and broil 2–3 minutes more. Turn and repeat on other side. Serve immediately.

6 servings

½ cup water
½ cup soy sauce
¼ cup Mr. Boston Ginger-Flavored Brandy
¼ cup sliced green onion
1 clove garlic, minced
1 teaspoon grated fresh ginger
2½ pounds swordfish

SOLE LUNAY

Combine cognac and anisette; drizzle ¼ cup over fillets and let stand 5 minutes. Combine nuts, crumbs, parsley, salt, and pepper and coat fish with mixture. Place in buttered baking pan. Combine butter with remaining 2 tablespoons liquor mixture. Drizzle over fish. Bake in preheated 400°F. oven 15–18 minutes.

6 servings

3 tablespoons Rémy Martin V.S.O.P. Cognac
3 tablespoons Mr. Boston Anisette
2 pounds sole fillets
1 cup finely chopped nuts or pine nuts
½ cup fine, dry bread crumbs
¼ cup chopped parsley
1 teaspoon salt
¼ teaspoon white pepper
⅓ cup melted butter

ANISETTE STEAMED FISH

¼ cup Mr. Boston
  Anisette
 1 cup water
¼ cup lemon juice
 2 tablespoons butter
1½ cups thinly sliced
  onion
¾ cup thinly sliced
  celery
 1 clove garlic, minced
2½ pounds whole red
  snapper, sea bass, or
  striped bass
 1 lemon, thinly sliced
1-2 tablespoons butter,
  softened
½ teaspoon salt
½ teaspoon white
  pepper

Combine anisette, water, lemon juice, butter, onion, celery, and garlic in large skillet; bring to a boil. Reduce heat and simmer 10 minutes. Add fish, cover, and cook over low heat 20 minutes. Remove skin, head, and tail from fish. Deco-rate with lemon slices. Strain cooking liquid, pressing vegetables to extract juices. Whisk in 1–2 tablespoons soft butter, salt, and pepper. Ladle sauce over fish to serve.

4–6 servings

Anisette Steamed Fish

Oriental Shrimp

CURRIED SHRIMP BALLS WITH COCONUT CREAM

Combine shrimp, Scotch, curry powder, and salt; mix thoroughly. Drop shrimp balls by tablespoonfuls into hot oil and brown on both sides, about 5 minutes. Remove shrimp balls from oil with slotted spoon, drain, and keep warm. Cook onion and coconut in butter over low heat about 5 minutes. Add cream and pepper; simmer 5–10 minutes. Stir in shrimp balls and heat through before serving. Accompany with rice.

4 servings

1 pound raw shrimp, shelled, deveined, and chopped
3 tablespoons Glenmore Scotch
1 tablespoon curry powder
¾ teaspoon salt
2 tablespoons vegetable oil
1 cup chopped onion
½ cup shredded coconut
3 tablespoons butter
1 cup heavy cream
¼ teaspoon cayenne pepper

SWORDSTEAK SKEWERS

Combine lemon juice, Scotch, oil, sugar, and seasonings; stir to blend. Pour mixture over fish and marinate 3 hours. Thread fish cubes alternately with tomatoes, zucchini or cucumber chunks, and mushrooms onto 12 skewers. Brush on marinade and broil 4–5 minutes.

6 servings

¾ cup lemon juice
¼ cup Desmond & Duff Deluxe Scotch
¼ cup oil
2 teaspoons sugar
2 teaspoons basil
2 teaspoons salt
½ teaspoon pepper
2 pounds swordfish, cut into 1-inch cubes
24 cherry tomatoes
24 one-inch chunks zucchini or cucumber,
12 small mushrooms

SOUTH SEAS FISH SAUTÉ

¼ **cup flour**
1 **teaspoon salt**
¼ **teaspoon white pepper**
6 **six-ounce red snapper, grouper, or yellowtail fillets**
6 **tablespoons butter**
3 **slightly underripe bananas, cut in half lengthwise**
3 **tomatoes, skinned, seeded, and chopped**
¼ **cup Mr. Boston Triple Sec**
3 **tablespoons Mr. Boston Five Star Brandy**
1 **cup fish stock (or ½ cup clam juice and ½ cup water)**

Stir together flour, salt, and pepper. Dust fish with flour mixture. Brown in 3 tablespoons butter on both sides and continue cooking over low heat until done; set aside. Cook banana halves in 2 tablespoons butter over low heat, 4–5 minutes. Remove and place one half on each fish fillet. Cook tomatoes in pan juices 1–2 minutes, add Triple Sec and brandy, and cook over medium-high heat 1–2 minutes. Stir in fish stock and cook over high heat until liquid is reduced by half, about 5 minutes. Add remaining butter to sauce and stir to blend. Serve over fish.

6 servings

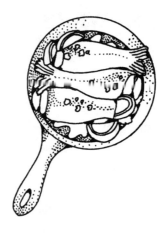

ORIENTAL SHRIMP

Stir together flour, baking powder, and salt. Gradually add warm water, beating with a wire whisk until smooth. Heat two inches of oil in a heavy-bottomed pan. Dip shrimp into batter and drop into oil. Cook for three minutes or until golden brown. Drain and serve immediately with Ginger Dipping Sauce.

6 servings

1 cup flour
1 teaspoon baking powder
¼ teaspoon salt
1 cup warm water
2 pounds shrimp, shelled and deveined
Ginger Dipping Sauce (see below)

Ginger Dipping Sauce

Combine first three ingredients in saucepan. Heat to a boil, lower heat, and simmer 4–5 minutes. Remove from heat. Place ginger in the bottom of serving bowl; add sauce and garnish with radish slices.

½ cup Mr. Boston Ginger-Flavored Brandy
½ cup soy sauce
½ cup beef broth
¼–½ teaspoon grated fresh ginger

GINGER-LIMED PIKE

¼ cup flour
1 teaspoon salt
¼ teaspoon white pepper
4 six-ounce pike fillets
Lime juice
¼ cup butter, softened
1 tablespoon grated
   fresh ginger
1 tablespoon minced
   green onion, white
   part only
½ teaspoon grated lime
   peel
2 tablespoons Mr.
   Boston Ginger-
   Flavored Brandy
½ teaspoon salt
⅛ teaspoon pepper

Stir together flour, salt, and pepper. Lightly dust fish with flour mixture. Sauté or broil 3–4 minutes on each side or until done. Squeeze fresh lime juice over fish; keep warm. Combine butter, ginger, onion, lime peel, brandy, salt, and pepper; heat mixture until butter starts to brown. Remove immediately and pour over fish.

4 servings

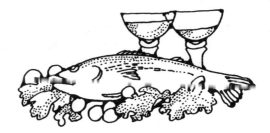

WHISKEY-SAUCED FISH

Melt butter in whiskey over medium heat. Add wine, stock, tomatoes, mushrooms, parsley, tarragon, and garlic; bring to a boil, reduce to medium heat, and cook until mixture thickens slightly, 20–25 minutes. Add lemon juice, salt, and pepper. Reduce heat to low, add fish and simmer until fish flakes easily, 12–15 minutes.

4 servings

3 tablespoons butter
¼ cup Old Thompson American Whiskey
½ cup dry white wine
½ cup fish stock (or ¼ cup clam broth and ¼ cup water)
1½ cups chopped, seeded tomatoes
1½ cups sliced mushrooms
1 tablespoon chopped parsley
1 teaspoon tarragon
1 clove garlic, minced
2 teaspoons lemon juice
1 teaspoon salt
¼ teaspoon pepper
2 pounds sea bass, grouper, or red snapper fillets

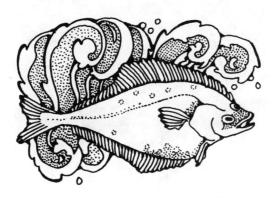

VENETIAN STEW

1 leek, chopped
1 clove garlic, minced
2 tablespoons olive oil
3 tomatoes, peeled,
  seeded, and chopped
1 cup water
½ cup dry white wine
¼ cup parsley
2 teaspoons salt
½ teaspoon sugar
½ teaspoon pepper
2 pounds flounder fillets
3 tablespoons Mr.
  Boston Five Star
  Brandy
Parmesan cheese, grated

Cook leek and garlic in olive oil until tender, about 5 minutes. Add tomatoes, wine, water, parsley, salt, sugar, and pepper. Simmer 1 hour. Add fish and continue simmering 15–20 minutes or until fish flakes easily. Stir in brandy. Sprinkle with cheese just before serving.

6 servings

SEAFOOD WITH VEGETABLES AND WHISKEY

Split lobster tails and crab legs lengthwise in shells. Cook chopped vegetables in 4 tablespoons butter until tender. Season with salt and pepper. Add lobster, crab, and Scotch. Hold lighted match close to surface so that Scotch flames. When flame dies, stir in bay leaves, garlic, thyme, and wine. Cook over medium heat until wine has evaporated, 10–15 minutes. Pour in fish stock and simmer 10 minutes. Remove lobster and crabmeat from shells; chop and reserve. Return shells to liquid. Stir in scallops, remaining butter, cognac, and parsley; simmer 10 minutes. Remove shells, stir in chopped lobster and crabmeat, and heat through. Serve immediately.

6–8 servings

- 1 pound lobster tails
- 1 pound Alaskan king crab legs
- ¾ cup chopped carrots
- ⅓ cup chopped celery
- ¼ cup chopped onion
- 1 chopped leek
- 1 chopped shallot
- ½ cup butter
- 1 teaspoon salt
- ¼ teaspoon pepper
- ¼ cup Desmond & Duff Deluxe Scotch Whiskey
- 2 bay leaves
- 1 minced garlic clove
- ¼ teaspoon thyme
- 1 cup Lawrence Fumé Blanc
- 2 cups fish stock (or 1 cup each of clam juice and water)
- 1 pound scallops
- 2 tablespoons Rémy Martin V.S.O.P Cognac
- 1 tablespoon chopped parsley

ALL PURPOSE FISH POACHING LIQUOR

2 quarts chicken broth
1 onion, coarsely
    chopped
2 stalks celery, sliced
¼ cup chopped parsley
1 tablespoon salt
3 bay leaves
1 teaspoon thyme
¾ cup Mr. Boston
    Apricot Flavored
    Brandy
3–5 pounds fish

Bring broth, vegetables, and seasonings to boil; reduce heat and simmer 40–60 minutes. Stir in brandy and bring to boil. Reduce heat; add fish and simmer 10–15 minutes or until fish flakes easily.

Makes 2 quarts

CHICKEN IN CHAMPAGNE SAUCE

½ cup flour
2 teaspoons salt
½ teaspoon pepper
2 frying chickens (2½–3
    pounds each) cut up
¼ cup butter
2 cups Torre Dei Cont
    Asti Spumante
½ teaspoon freshly
    grated lemon peel
2 tablespoons cornstarch
2 tablespoons water
2 tablespoons heavy
    cream
1 tablespoon chopped
    parsley (optional)

Stir together flour, salt, and pepper. Lightly dust chicken with flour mixture. Cook in butter on both sides until golden; drain fat. Add wine and lemon peel. Simmer, covered, 35–40 minutes. Remove chicken to serving platter and keep warm. Combine cornstarch and water; stir into pan juices. Cook over medium heat until smooth and thickened, stirring constantly. Stir in cream and parsley. Serve sauce over chicken.

8 servings

PLUMMED CHICKEN

Cook onion in 3 tablespoons butter over medium heat until tender. Add plums, increase heat, and cook 2–3 minutes until plums are lightly browned. Place onions and plums in 4-quart ovenproof baking dish; sprinkle with seasonings. Brown chicken on both sides in remaining butter; place over plum mixture in baking dish. Pour broth and brandy over top. Cover and bake in preheated 350°F. oven 45–50 minutes. Cover may be removed during last 10 minutes of cooking, if desired.

8 servings

1½ **cups sliced onion**
6 **tablespoons butter**
12 **fresh plums, halved and pitted (or one 28-ounce can plums)**
1 **tablespoon allspice**
2 **teaspoons salt**
½ **teaspoon pepper**
2 **frying chickens (2½–3 pounds each), cut up**
½ **cup chicken broth**
¼ **cup Mr. Boston Cherry Flavored Brandy**

ANISETTE CHICKEN

Brown chicken breasts in butter on both sides. Remove chicken from pan and keep warm. Reduce heat to low; add garlic, celery, onion, salt, and pepper to pan juices and cook 5 minutes. Add broth, cognac, and anisette; bring to a boil. Reduce heat, return chicken to pan and simmer 30–35 minutes or until chicken is tender. Serve chicken with sauce.

4–6 servings

3 **chicken breasts, split**
¼ **cup butter**
1 **clove garlic, minced**
½ **cup sliced celery**
¼ **cup chopped green onion**
1 **teaspoon salt**
½ **teaspoon pepper**
1½ **cups chicken broth**
2 **tablespoons Rémy Martin V.S.O.P. Cognac**
2 **tablespoons Mr. Boston Anisette**

※-※-※-※-※
MINT FRIED CHICKEN

2 frying chickens (2½–3
   pounds each), cut up
¾ cup Mr. Boston Crème
   de Menthe (white)
1 cup flour
1 tablespoon salt
1 teaspoon pepper
1 teaspoon dried mint
¼ cup butter

Sprinkle chicken with ¼ cup crème de menthe; let stand 5 minutes. Stir together flour and seasonings; coat chicken pieces with mixture, shaking off excess. Brown chicken on all sides in butter. Reduce heat to low, cover, and cook until tender, 25–30 minutes. Heat remaining ½ cup crème de menthe, sprinkle over chicken, and flambé. After flame dies, serve immediately.

8 servings

※-※-※-※-※
GINGER CREAM CHICKEN

3 tablespoons Mr.
   Boston Ginger
   Flavored Brandy
2 eggs, beaten
¾ cup flour
1 teaspoon ginger
1 teaspoon salt
½ teaspoon pepper
3 whole chicken breasts,
   halved, boned, and
   pounded to ¼-inch
   thick
½ cup butter
1 tablespoon cornstarch
¾ cup chicken broth
¾ cup half-and-half
1 clove garlic, minced

Blend 1 tablespoon brandy with eggs until smooth. Stir together flour, ½ teaspoon ginger, salt, and pepper. Dip chicken in egg batter and coat with flour mixture. Brown chicken on both sides in ¼ cup butter and cook until done, 3–5 minutes on each side. Remove chicken from pan and keep warm. Combine cornstarch and ¼ cup chicken broth; blend until smooth. Cook cornstarch mixture together with remaining ½ cup chicken broth, ¼ cup butter, 2 tablespoons brandy, ½ teaspoon ginger, half-and-half, and garlic until smooth and thickened, stirring constantly. Season to taste with salt and pepper. Serve over chicken.

4–6 servings

CORNISH HENS WITH GREEN APPLES

Cook bacon and onion in skillet until bacon is brown but not crisp and onion is soft. Add garlic and cook 2–3 minutes longer. Remove bacon-onion mixture and reserve. Stir together flour, 1 teaspoon salt, and pepper. Lightly dust hens with flour mixture. Brown in pan drippings. Place hens in baking pan. Sprinkle reserved mixture and remaining teaspoon salt over top. Cook apple slices in butter and Amaretto Di Saronno, over high heat, until apples are browned. Place apples and juices in baking pan with hens. Bake, uncovered, in preheated 350°F. oven 45–50 minutes or until hens are tender.

4 servings

¼ pound bacon, diced
½ cup finely chopped onion
1 clove garlic, minced
¼ cup flour
2 teaspoons salt
¼ teaspoon pepper
2 Cornish hens, split
2 tart green apples, unpeeled and sliced
2 tablespoons butter
¼ cup Amaretto di Saronno

CORNISH HENS WITH APPLE-GRAPE STUFFING

Combine bread cubes, fruits, and celery. Blend sour cream, ½ cup butter, 3 tablespoons brandy, and seasonings. Stir into dry mixture; blend thoroughly. Stuff 1–1½ cups into each hen. Place any remaining stuffing in separate casserole. Combine remaining ½ cup butter and 2 tablespoons brandy; brush over hens. Bake in preheated 375°F. oven 35–40 minutes or until tender, brushing hens with butter mixture once during cooking. Bake extra stuffing, covered, 20–25 minutes.

6–8 servings

3 cups dry, seasoned bread cubes
2½ cups chopped red apple
2 cups green grapes, halved
1 cup chopped celery
1 cup sour cream
1 cup butter, melted
5 tablespoons Mr. Boston Five Star Brandy
1 teaspoon ground cinnamon
1 teaspoon salt
½ teaspoon white pepper
6 Cornish hens

CORNISH HENS WITH BING CHERRY SAUCE

1 sixteen-ounce can dark
   sweet cherries,
   drained; reserve juice
2 teaspoons cornstarch
½ cup beef broth
3 tablespoons
   Mandarine Napoleon
2 tablespoons Mr.
   Boston Cherry
   Flavored Brandy
1 tablespoon lemon juice
½ teaspoon allspice
1 tablespoon butter
4 Cornish hens, split

Blend 1 tablespoon cherry juice with cornstarch. Combine with remaining cherry juice, broth, Mandarine Napoleon, brandy, lemon juice, and allspice. Bring mixture to a boil and cook over high heat 2 minutes, stirring constantly. Reduce heat to low and simmer 5 minutes. Stir in cherries. Remove from heat and blend in butter. Place cornish hens in roasting pan with rack. Brush cherry sauce over hens and bake in preheated 350°F. oven 45–50 minutes or until tender. Brush hens 2–3 times during baking. Serve with remaining sauce and cherries.

6–8 servings

TANGY TURKEY BREAST

1 cup butter
1⅓ tablespoons Mr.
   Boston Apricot
   Flavored Brandy
1¼ teaspoons red wine
   vinegar
1¼ teaspoons dried
   orange peel
1 teaspoon salt
¼ teaspoon white
   pepper
5–6 pounds turkey breast

Heat butter together with brandy, vinegar, orange peel, and seasonings. Reserve ½ cup, brushing remainder over turkey breast on rack in roasting pan. Bake in preheated 350°F. oven 1½–2 hours or until done, basting every 20–30 minutes with pan juices. Let cooked breast stand 15 minutes before slicing. Serve with reserved brandy butter.

8–10 servings

VEAL- AND HAM-STUFFED TURKEY

Combine ground meats, onion, bread crumbs, 2 tablespoons brandy, and seasonings; blend thoroughly. Place about 2 tablespoons of mixture in center of each cutlet. Roll each cutlet up around stuffing and secure with toothpick. Brown rolled cutlets on all sides in butter. Add broth and wine; cover and simmer 30 minutes. Remove cutlets from pan and keep warm. Blend water and flour until smooth. Stir into pan juices and cook until thickened, stirring constantly. Return rolls to pan; heat thoroughly. Heat remaining 2 tablespoons brandy, drizzle over rolls, and flambé. When flame dies, serve immediately.

6 servings

⅓ **pound ground ham**
⅓ **pound ground veal**
½ **cup chopped onion**
⅓ **cup soft bread crumbs**
¼ **cup Mr. Boston Five Star Brandy**
½ **teaspoon allspice**
½ **teaspoon nutmeg**
½ **teaspoon salt**
¼ **teaspoon pepper**
6 **four-ounce turkey cutlets, pounded to ¼-inch thickness**
3–4 **tablespoons butter**
1 **cup chicken broth**
½ **cup Lawrence Fumé Blanc**
2 **tablespoons water**
1 **tablespoon flour**

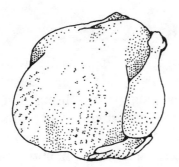

DUCK WITH APRICOTS

1 five- to six-pound duck
1 teaspoon salt
½ teaspoon pepper
1 sixteen-ounce can
   apricot halves,
   drained; reserve ½ cup
   juice
½ cup Mr. Boston
   Apricot Flavored
   Brandy
½ cup chicken broth
2 tablespoons Mr.
   Boston Triple Sec
1 tablespoon cornstarch
1 tablespoon water

Season duck with salt and pepper. Roast in preheated 350°F. oven 30 minutes. Prick skin and bake for another 1½ hours or until done. Remove from oven and keep warm. Drain fat from roasting pan. Add reserved apricot liquid and brandy to roasting pan; bring to a boil. Boil 1–2 minutes, stirring constantly. Transfer to saucepan. Add chicken broth and Triple Sec; simmer 10 minutes. Mix cornstarch and water; stir into simmering mixture. Continue cooking until thickened, stirring constantly. Strain sauce if necessary. Stir in apricot halves and heat thoroughly. Serve sauce over duck.

4 servings

ROAST DUCK CASSIS

1 five- to six-pound
   duck
1½ teaspoons thyme
1 teaspoon salt
½ teaspoon pepper
⅔ cup coarsely chopped
   onion
½ cup Mr. Boston
   Crème de Cassis
1 cup beef broth
Watercress for garnish

Season duck with thyme, salt, and pepper. Place onion on flat perforated rack in roasting pan; place duck on top. Bake in preheated 450°F. oven 15 minutes. Reduce heat to 375°F., prick skin, and bake 1½ hours or until done. Remove duck from roasting pan and keep warm. Drain fat from pan and place onion with defatted pan drippings into saucepan. Add crème de cassis, bring to a boil, and boil 1 minute. Add beef broth, return to a boil and cook over medium heat about 10 minutes; strain. Serve sauce with duck and garnish with watercress.

4 servings

DUCK WITH ORANGE PRUNE SAUCE

Season duck with 1 teaspoon salt and ¼ teaspoon pepper. Roast in preheated 350°F. oven 30 minutes. Prick skin and bake 1 hour and 15 minutes. Combine peels, fruit juices, cognac, and Triple Sec; bring to a boil. Cook over medium heat until liquid is reduced to 2 cups, about 15 minutes. Add prunes, reduce heat and simmer 10 minutes. Combine cornstarch and water; stir into simmering liquid. Cook until clear and thickened, 3–4 minutes, stirring constantly. Add remaining 1 teaspoon salt and ¼ teaspoon pepper. Spoon ½ cup sauce over duck and bake 15 additional minutes. Serve with orange sections and remaining sauce.

4 servings

1 five-to six-pound duck
2 teaspoons salt
½ teaspoon white pepper
1½ tablespoons freshly grated orange peel
1 tablespoon freshly grated lemon peel
2 cups orange juice
⅓ cup lemon juice
¼ cup Rémy Martin V.S.O.P. Cognac
¼ cup Mr. Boston Triple Sec
12–15 whole pitted prunes
1 tablespoon cornstarch
1 tablespoon water
2 oranges, sectioned and seeded

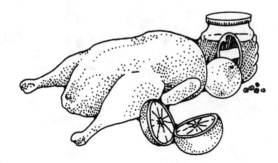

BAVARIAN APPLE POT ROAST

3 tart cooking apples, peeled, cored, and sliced
½ cup Mr. Boston Five Star Brandy
½ teaspoon ginger
½ teaspoon ground cloves
4 pounds pot roast
2 tablespoons butter
1 medium onion, sliced
1 teaspoon sugar
2 tablespoons flour
½ cup unsweetened apple juice
½ cup beef broth
2 teaspoons salt
½ teaspoon pepper

Combine apple slices, brandy, ginger, and cloves; stir to coat apple slices. Set aside. Brown pot roast in butter on both sides; remove roast and set aside. Cook onion with sugar in drippings until golden. Stir in flour and gradually blend in apple juice, beef broth, salt, pepper, and apple-brandy mixture; bring to a boil. Return roast to pot, reduce heat, cover, and simmer 2–2½ hours or until roast is tender. Remove roast, cool slightly, and slice. Bring sauce to a boil and cook over medium heat until thickened, about 15 minutes. Serve over roast.

6–8 servings

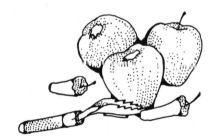

Veal Roast with Sage Dressing
Braised Lamb Shanks au Vin Rouge

꿏-꿏-꿏-꿏-꿏

FLANK STEAK SUPREME

Cut pocket in the flank steak; score surfaces. Combine brandy, ½ cup onion, soy sauce, oil, salt, and ¼ teaspoon pepper; mix well. Marinate steak in mixture at least 3 hours. Sauté ½ cup onion, mushrooms, and celery in butter until tender. Stir in broth, thyme, and ½ teaspoon pepper; bring mixture to a boil. Remove from heat and stir in bread cubes. Remove steak from marinade. Fill pocket with stuffing. Pin sides together with metal skewers if necessary. Broil or grill 5–7 minutes on each side. Slice diagonally to serve.

4–6 servings

1½–2 pounds flank steak
1 cup Mr. Boston Peach Flavored Brandy
1 cup chopped onion
⅓ cup soy sauce
¼ cup oil
¼ teaspoon salt
¾ teaspoon pepper
¼ pound mushrooms, sliced
¼ cup chopped celery
1 tablespoon butter
½ cup beef broth or water
1 teaspoon thyme
2 cups dry bread cubes

꿏-꿏-꿏-꿏-꿏

SIRLOIN PATTIES ELEGANTE

Combine sirloin and salt; shape into 6 patties. Press 1 teaspoon peppercorns, evenly spread, into each patty. Broil on both sides to desired doneness. Remove from broiler and keep warm. Cook mushrooms in butter over medium heat 3–4 minutes. Stir in cognac, Worcestershire sauce, and lemon juice; continue cooking 2–3 minutes. Remove from heat and stir in cream. Serve sauce over patties.

6 servings

2¼ pounds ground sirloin
1½ teaspoons salt
2 tablespoons whole black peppercorns, cracked
½ pound mushrooms, sliced
2 tablespoons butter
¼ cup Rémy Martin V.S.O.P. Cognac
2 teaspoons Worcestershire sauce
2 teaspoons lemon juice
2 tablespoons cream

43

PRIME RIB ROAST WITH YORKSHIRE PUDDING AND SCOTCH GRAVY

Prime Rib Roast

6½–7 pounds prime rib roast (first 3 ribs), trimmed and at room temperature
¼ cup vegetable oil
½ teaspoon coarsely cracked black pepper

Rub roast with 1 tablespoon oil and press pepper into fat. Heat remaining oil in roasting pan. Set roast in hot oil and bake in preheated 375°F. oven 15 minutes per pound or to internal temperature of 140°F. for rare meat and 18 minutes per pound or to 160°F. for medium meat. Baste roast with pan juices every 20–30 minutes during cooking. Remove roast, drain fat, reserving both fat and remaining pan juices. Let cooked roast stand 15 minutes before carving. Serve with Yorkshire Pudding and Scotch Gravy.

8–10 servings

Yorkshire Pudding

2 cups flour
1 teaspoon salt
2 cups water
1 cup milk
4 eggs
Reserved beef fat and melted shortening to make 1 cup
2 tablespoons Desmond & Duff Deluxe Scotch

Sift together flour and salt. Combine water and milk. Beat eggs with 1¼ cups liquid until smooth. Make a well in center of flour mixture and pour in egg mixture. Whisk liquid into flour to make a smooth batter, adding enough additional liquid to make a batter the consistency of heavy cream. Mix fat and Scotch together in 9 × 13-inch pan. Heat in preheated 450°F. oven 5–8 minutes or until fat is very hot. Stir batter and pour into pan all at once. Bake in preheated 450°F. oven until puffed and golden, 35–40 minutes. Serve immediately.

To make individual Yorkshire puddings, prepare batter as directed above. Stir Scotch into fat and place about 1 tablespoon of mixture in each of 12 muffin cups. Fill cups ¾ full with batter and bake in preheated 450°F. oven 15–20 minutes or until puffed and golden. The pudding may be kept a few minutes in warm oven before serving.

Scotch Gravy

Add 1 cup broth to roasting pan with defatted drippings. Cook over medium heat, stirring constantly, until meat drippings are loosened from roasting pan. Pour mixture into saucepan. Blend Scotch and flour until smooth. Add ¼ cup broth and blend until smooth. Stir flour mixture and remaining broth into saucepan. Bring mixture to a boil, reduce heat, and cook, stirring constantly, until smooth and thickened slightly.

3 cups beef broth
3 tablespoons Desmond & Duff Deluxe Scotch
2 tablespoons flour

LONDON BROIL ORIENTAL

¾ cup pineapple juice
¼ cup Mr. Boston Ginger
   Flavored Brandy
3 tablespoons soy sauce
1 tablespoon sesame oil
1–2 cloves garlic, minced
2 pounds flank steak

Combine all liquid ingredients and garlic; stir to blend. Pour over steak and marinate in refrigerator overnight. Remove steak and broil to desired doneness. Heat marinade and serve as dipping sauce with steak.

4–6 servings

CALVES' LIVER WITH SAUCE CASSIS

½ cup plus 3
   tablespoons flour
1½ teaspoons salt
½ teaspoon pepper
2 pounds calves' liver,
   thinly sliced on
   diagonal
2 tablespoons oil
¼ cup butter
3 tablespoons minced
   shallots
1 cup beef broth
1 teaspoon
   Worcestershire sauce
½ cup Mr. Boston
   Crème de Cassis
1 tablespoon currants

Stir together ½ cup flour, salt, and pepper. Lightly dust liver with flour mixture. Brown liver, a little at a time, on both sides in oil and 2 tablespoons butter. Remove from skillet and keep warm. Clean out skillet; melt remaining butter and sauté shallots over low heat 2–3 minutes. Add remaining flour; cook and stir about 1 minute over medium heat. Add remaining ingredients and cook over low heat about 5 minutes, stirring constantly, until smooth and thickened. Serve sauce over calves' liver.

6 servings

HORSERADISH STEAK SAUCE

Cook bacon until crisp; remove and drain. Add mushrooms to skillet and cook over medium heat until golden. Stir in remaining ingredients; cook over medium heat about 5 minutes. Stir in bacon. Serve with steak.

Makes 1½ cups

¼ cup diced bacon
2 cups sliced fresh mushrooms
1 cup crème fraiche or sour cream
1 tablespoon Old Thompson American Whiskey
1 tablespoon prepared horseradish
¼ teaspoon salt

HORSERADISH CREAM

Blend all ingredients except cream until smooth. Fold into whipped cream. Chill 2–3 hours before serving. Serve with beef brisket, roast, or steak.

Makes 1 cup

¼ cup prepared horseradish
1 tablespoon Rémy Martin V.S.O.P. Cognac
2 teaspoons white wine vinegar
1 teaspoon dry mustard
1 teaspoon sugar
⅛ teaspoon salt
½ cup heavy cream, whipped

꿿꿿꿿꿿꿿

LIQUOR BUTTERS

Savory Scotch Butter

½ cup butter
2 anchovy fillets, minced
1 tablespoon Desmond & Duff Deluxe Scotch

Melt butter; blend in remaining ingredients. Serve with steak.

Lemon Garlic Butter

½ cup butter
2 cloves garlic, minced
1 tablespoon Yellowstone Mellow Mash
1 teaspoon fresh grated lemon peel

Melt butter; blend in remaining ingredients. Brush over chicken or turkey during cooking.

Apricot Orange Butter

½ cup butter
1 tablespoon Mr. Boston Apricot Flavored Brandy
1 teaspoon red wine vinegar
½ teaspoon grated dried orange peel
¼ teaspoon white pepper

Melt butter; blend in remaining ingredients. Brush over pork or turkey during cooking.

A Dilly of a Butter

Melt butter; blend in remaining ingredients. Serve over cooked fish.

½ cup butter
1 tablespoon Glenmore Gin
1 tablespoon fresh lemon juice
½ teaspoon dried dill weed

VEAL SCALLOPINI ROLLS

Cook bacon, onion, carrot, parsley, and garlic in 2 tablespoons butter over low heat, 5 minutes. Add Scotch, rosemary, and salt and cook until liquid has evaporated, about 3 minutes. Remove from heat. Spread 1 tablespoon of filling over each scallopini. Roll up and secure with wooden pick. Roll each in flour; shake off excess. Brown veal rolls in remaining 2 tablespoons butter on all sides. Reduce heat to medium-low and cook 5–7 minutes more, turning frequently until done.

4–6 servings

4 strips bacon, diced
1 cup minced onion
1 cup minced carrot
¼ cup chopped parsley
4 cloves garlic, minced
¼ cup butter
¼ cup Desmond & Duff Deluxe Scotch
½ teaspoon rosemary
¼ teaspoon salt
1½–2 pounds veal scallopini sliced into 8 pieces and pounded thin
Flour

PEACHES 'N' CREAMED VEAL

3 tablespoons flour
1 teaspoon salt
¼ teaspoon pepper
1½ pounds veal
   scallopini, sliced into
   6 pieces and pounded
   thin
3 tablespoons butter
½ cup Mr. Boston
   Peach Flavored
   Brandy
1½ cups heavy cream
2 tablespoons lemon
   juice
   Peach halves

Stir together flour, salt, and pepper. Lightly dust veal slices with flour mixture; shake off excess. Brown veal in butter, 2–3 pieces at a time, on both sides. Remove and keep warm. Add brandy to pan drippings and cook 1 minute, stirring constantly. Add cream and cook 10 minutes until sauce thickens slightly. Stir in lemon juice and season to taste with salt and pepper. Return veal to sauce and heat through. Arrange veal on bed of wild rice and garnish with peach halves. Serve immediately.

6 servings

VEAL WITH DIJON MUSTARD SAUCE

1½ pounds veal
   scallopini
¼ cup butter
¼ cup chopped green
   onion
1½ tablespoons flour
1½ cups half-and-half or
   light cream
2 tablespoons Dijon
   mustard
1½ tablespoons Mr.
   Boston Five Star
   Brandy
½ teaspoon salt
¼ teaspoon white
   pepper

Brown veal on both sides in butter, reduce heat, and cook to desired doneness. Remove and keep warm. Stir onions and flour into pan and cook 1–2 minutes. Add remaining ingredients and cook over medium heat until smooth and thickened, stirring constantly. Serve sauce with veal on bed of noodles.

6 servings

ANCHOVY-STUFFED VEAL CHOPS

Sauté onion, green pepper, and garlic in 2 tablespoons olive oil over medium heat until onion is translucent. Add anchovy paste, capers, and black olives and cook 2 minutes or until vegetables are tender. Stir in lemon juice, cook 1 minute more, and remove from heat. Stir in bread crumbs, egg, Parmesan cheese, and black pepper. Slice chops lengthwise to form pocket. Place about ⅓ cup stuffing in each chop. Brown chops on both sides in remaining 2 tablespoons oil. Remove meat, drain excess oil, add brandy and cook 1 minute. Add chicken broth and bring to a boil. Return veal chops to pan, reduce heat, cover, and simmer 30 minutes, turning chops once. Remove chops and keep warm. Continue cooking pan juices until reduced to 1 cup, about 10 minutes.

4 servings

⅓ cup chopped onion
⅓ cup chopped green pepper
1 clove garlic, minced
4 tablespoons olive oil
2 teaspoons anchovy paste
1 tablespoon chopped capers
1 tablespoon chopped black olives
2 teaspoons lemon juice
¼ cup fine, dry bread crumbs
1 egg, beaten
2 tablespoons grated Parmesan cheese
¼ teaspoon fresh ground black pepper
4 half-pound veal loin chops
⅓ cup Mr. Boston Five Star Brandy
⅔ cup chicken broth

VEAL ROAST WITH SAGE DRESSING

½ pound bulk pork
  sausage
½ cup chopped onion
½ cup chopped celery
3 cups dried bread
  cubes
2 tablespoons chopped
  parsley
1 egg
1 teaspoon sage*
1¼ teaspoons salt
6 tablespoons kümmel
3 pounds boneless veal
  shoulder roast
2 tablespoons butter,
  melted
¼ teaspoon pepper

Cook sausage over medium heat about 5 minutes; add onion and celery. Cook until vegetables are tender, about 8 minutes. Combine pork mixture with bread cubes and parsley. Add egg, sage, ½ teaspoon salt, and 3 tablespoons kümmel; mix well. Flatten veal shoulder. Spread stuffing over meat, roll up, and secure with string. Combine butter with remaining kümmel and seasonings; brush over roast. Bake, covered, in preheated 325°F. oven 1½ hours or until tender. Baste 2–3 times during cooking.

6 servings

*Use fresh sage for better flavor.

VEAL KIDNEYS WITH GIN

Brown kidney slices in oil over high heat, a few at a time. Sprinkle with salt and pepper. Remove from skillet and drain. Cook bacon over medium-low heat 1–2 minutes. Add shallots and continue cooking until bacon is crisp. Pour gin over shallots and bacon and flambé. When flame dies, stir in flour and cook, stirring constantly, 1–2 minutes. Gradually add beef broth and wine, stirring constantly, until smooth. Add seasonings and mushrooms and simmer 5–10 minutes, stirring occasionally, until thickened. Return kidneys to pan and heat thoroughly.

4–6 servings

1½ **pounds veal kidneys, cleaned and cut into ½-inch slices**
3 **tablespoons oil**
1 **teaspoon salt**
¼ **teaspoon pepper**
2 **strips bacon, diced**
2 **tablespoons minced shallots**
¼ **cup Glenmore Gin**
1½ **tablespoons flour**
¾ **cup beef broth**
⅓ **cup red wine**
¼ **teaspoon thyme**
3 **juniper berries, crushed and chopped (optional)**
1 **cup sliced mushrooms**

ORANGE BRANDIED LEG OF LAMB

Rub lamb with salt, pepper, and garlic. Bake in preheated 350°F. oven 1½–2 hours to desired doneness. Combine orange juice and peel and Triple Sec in saucepan. Cook over medium heat until reduced by half, 8–10 minutes. Reduce heat to low, whisk in butter and mustard, and season to taste with salt and pepper. Serve sauce over sliced lamb.

6 servings

1 **boneless leg of lamb**
2 **teaspoons salt**
½ **teaspoon pepper**
2 **cloves garlic, minced**
2 **cups orange juice**
2 **tablespoons fresh grated orange peel**
⅔ **cup Mr. Boston Triple Sec**
¼ **cup butter, softened**
2 **tablespoons Dijon-style mustard**

SWEET AND SOUR LAMB

1 cup thinly sliced onion
2 tablespoons butter
¼ cup Mr. Boston Crème de Menthe (white)
¼ cup vinegar
1 tablespoon sugar
2 teaspoons lemon juice
½ cup beef broth
½ teaspoon rosemary
6 lamb chops

Cook onion in butter over low heat until onion is tender, 10–15 minutes. Blend crème de menthe, vinegar, sugar, and lemon juice; add to onions and simmer until mixture looks syrupy, about 10 minutes.

Stir in beef broth and rosemary and simmer 15 minutes. Broil or sauté lamb chops to desired doneness. Serve with sauce.

4–6 servings

LAMB RIB CHOPS WITH COFFEE BRANDY CREAM SAUCE

½ cup Mr. Boston Coffee Flavored Brandy
½ cup beef broth
1 cup heavy cream
12 lamb rib chops

Bring coffee brandy to a boil. Add beef broth and heavy cream; blend well. Continue to cook over medium heat, stirring occasionally, until reduced to 1 cup, 20–25 minutes.

(Sauce thickens slightly and darkens in color.) Broil lamb chops to desired doneness. Serve with sauce.

4 servings

BRAISED LAMB SHANKS AU VIN ROUGE

Stir together flour, salt, and pepper. Rub shanks with flour mixture. Brown lamb in butter and oil on all sides. Remove from pan and set aside. Add onion to pan and cook until tender. Add carrot, celery, and garlic and cook 2–3 minutes. Stir in wine, Mandarine Napoleon, and seasonings. Add shanks, cover, and simmer over low heat 3 hours.

4 servings

- 3 tablespoons flour
- ¼ teaspoon salt
- ⅛ teaspoon pepper
- 4 lamb shanks
- 2 tablespoons butter
- 2 tablespoons oil
- 1½ cups chopped onion
- 1 cup chopped carrots
- 1 cup chopped celery
- 1 clove garlic, minced
- ¾ cup red wine
- ¼ cup Mandarine Napoleon
- 2 sprigs parsley
- 1 teaspoon thyme
- 1 bay leaf
- 1 teaspoon marjoram

FRUIT-STUFFED PORK LOIN WITH APRICOT GLAZE

Cook apricots and prunes in brandy 3 minutes, cover, and let stand 1 hour. Unroll pork loin, fat side down. Make a deep lengthwise cut into meaty part to make pocket for fruits. Drain fruit, reserving liquid. Fill pocket, alternating apricots and prunes. Roll up meat and secure with string. Rub meat with salt and ginger. Roast meat in preheated 325°F. oven for 2 hours or until it reaches an internal temperature of 170°F. Blend reserved apricot juice, apricot preserves, and soy sauce; brush over roast occasionally during roasting.

8–10 servings

- ½ cup dried apricots
- 12 pitted prunes
- ⅔ cup Mr. Boston Apricot Flavored Brandy
- 4 pounds boneless rolled pork loin
- 1 teaspoon salt
- ¼ teaspoon ground ginger
- ½ cup apricot preserves
- 1 teaspoon soy sauce

PORK TENDERLOIN WITH CREAM

¼ cup flour
2 teaspoons salt
½ teaspoon pepper
8 half-inch-thick slices
  pork tenderloin, lightly
  pounded
2–3 tablespoons butter
⅔ cup Balfour Cream
  Sherry
⅔ cup heavy cream
2 egg yolks

Stir together flour, salt, and pepper. Lightly dust pork with flour mixture. Brown in butter on both sides; reduce heat and cook 5–7 minutes on each side or until cooked through. Remove pork from pan and keep warm. Drain fat from pan. Add sherry to defatted pan and cook over medium heat 1–2 minutes. Combine cream and egg yolks and whisk into sherry. Reduce heat to low and cook just until thickened, stirring constantly. Serve over pork slices.

6–8 servings

CRANBERRY-GLAZED RIBS

9 pounds pork loin back
  ribs
1 cup cranberry-orange
  relish
½ cup Desmond & Duff
  Scotch
⅓ cup soy sauce
3 tablespoons sugar
2 tablespoons prepared
  mustard
2 cloves garlic, minced
¾ teaspoon ground
  ginger

Cook ribs in covered pan in preheated 350°F. oven 60 minutes. Blend remaining ingredients until smooth. Remove cover from ribs; baste liberally with mixture and return to 400°F. oven. Cook 20 minutes more, basting with glaze once during cooking.

6 servings

FRIED PORK AND CABBAGE

Cook bacon until crisp; remove from pan, drain, and cut into ½-inch pieces. Saute onion and garlic in bacon drippings. Add pork and brown on both sides; remove from pan and keep warm. Add cabbage, kümmel, and seasonings; cook over medium heat, stirring occasionally, until cabbage is soft. Return pork and bacon to skillet, cover, and cook 10 minutes. Combine sour cream and gin or vodka, stir into cabbage mixture, and heat through. Serve immediately.

4–6 servings

4 slices bacon
½ cup finely chopped onion
1 garlic clove, minced
1½ pounds pork tenderloin medallions
1 small head cabbage (1–1½ pounds), shredded
2 tablespoons kümmel
1 tablespoon paprika
2 teaspoons sugar
1 teaspoon salt
½ teaspoon black pepper
½ cup sour cream
2 tablespoons Glenmore Gin or Vodka

SWEDISH PORK CHOPS

1 tart green apple, sliced
½ cup Mr. Boston Apple-
  Flavored Brandy
6 half-inch-thick pork
  chops
½ cup sliced mushrooms
¼ cup sliced green onion
¼ cup diced bacon
1 tablespoon butter
½ cup crème fraîche
½ teaspoon caraway
  seeds
1 teaspoon salt

Marinate apple slices in ¼ cup brandy 15 minutes. Pan broil pork chops on both sides until brown and place in ovenproof baking dish. Drain excess fat from skillet. Add mushrooms, onion, and bacon and cook over medium heat until bacon is not quite crisp. Add remaining brandy and cook, stirring constantly, 2–3 minutes. Pour juices over chops, leaving small amount in skillet. Add butter and marinated apple slices; cook over medium-high heat, stirring constantly, until apple slices are golden brown, about 5 minutes. Remove from heat and blend in crème fraîche and caraway seeds. Place apples around chops, sprinkle chops with salt, and pour pan juices over top. Cover and cook in preheated 350°F. oven 20 minutes. Remove cover and cook 10 minutes more.

4–6 servings

PORK LOIN JUBILEE

3 pounds pork loin roast
¼ cup water
1 tablespoon cornstarch
¼ cup tangerine juice
¼ cup lemon juice
2 tablespoons brown
  sugar
3 tablespoons
  Mandarine Napoleon
1 tablespoon grated
  tangerine peel

Roast pork in preheated 350°F. oven 1½ hours or to an internal temperature of 170°F. Remove to platter and keep warm. Drain all but 1 tablespoon fat from roasting pan. Combine water and cornstarch, stir into pan drippings and bring to a boil, stirring constantly, until mixture thickens slightly. Stir in tangerine and lemon juices and brown sugar; boil 1 minute. Remove from heat and stir in Mandarine Napoleon and tangerine peel. Pour sauce over roast; garnish with parsley and tangerine sections.

6 servings

Fruit-Stuffed Pork Loin with Apricot Glaze

Gingered Green Beans and Peppers

Side Dishes

Of all foods, side dishes lend themselves most readily to cooking with spirits. Delicate in nature, they usually reach the table after simmering, poaching, boiling, or other light processing. Spirits preserve the integrity of the original ingredients while adding something special.

Fruits and vegetables, in particular, welcome the robust contribution of bottled spirits, combining it with their own juices to make something enticingly new.

GINGERED GREEN BEANS AND PEPPERS

Cook green beans in salted water 5–7 minutes. Drain beans and refresh under cold water. Stir fry green beans and peppers in butter 5–6 minutes. Add brandy and cook until brandy has evaporated. Season to taste with salt and pepper. Serve with poultry or fish.

6 servings

2 pounds fresh whole green beans
2 red peppers, in julienne strips
3 tablespoons butter
½ cup Mr. Boston Ginger Flavored Brandy
Salt
Pepper

VEGETABLES AMARETTO

Place eggplant in colander and sprinkle with ½ teaspoon salt; let drain 25–30 minutes. Pat dry with paper towels. Cook pepper, onion, celery, parsnips, and garlic in butter and Amaretto di Saronno 5 minutes. Add tomatoes, eggplant, bay leaves, remaining ½ teaspoon salt, and pepper. Cook over medium heat 15 minutes. Sprinkle with parsley. Serve immediately with pork, lamb, or chicken.

6 servings

2 cups peeled, cubed eggplant
1 teaspoon salt
2 cups chopped green pepper
1 cup chopped onion
1 cup chopped celery
4 parsnips, in julienne strips
1 clove garlic, minced
3 tablespoons butter
½ cup Amaretto di Saronno
2 cups chopped tomatoes
2 bay leaves
¼ teaspoon pepper
3 tablespoons chopped parsley

GLAZED CARROTS AND BANANAS

2½ cups diagonally
  sliced carrots
2 tablespoons butter
¼ cup Mr. Boston Triple
  Sec
½ teaspoon salt
¼ cup chopped parsley
2 underripe bananas,
  sliced diagonally

Cook carrots in boiling water 8–10 minutes; drain. Combine carrots with butter, Triple Sec, salt, and parsley in saucepan; cook, stirring occasionally, until carrots are glazed. Add bananas; heat thoroughly. Serve immediately with pork or poultry.

4 servings

VEGETABLE MEDLEY

4 carrots, cut into
  2-inch julienne strips
4 parsnips, cut into
  2-inch julienne strips
4 stalks celery, cut into
  2-inch julienne strips
2 tablespoons butter,
  melted
½ cup Balfour Cream
  Sherry
1½ teaspoons salt
¼–½ teaspoon pepper
2 tablespoons chopped
  parsley
2 teaspoons lemon juice

Place vegetables in glass baking dish. Blend remaining ingredients and pour over vegetables. Cover and bake in preheated 375°F. oven for 20–25 minutes until tender, yet firm. Stir to blend before serving.

4 servings

MANDARIN CARROTS IN CREAM

Cook carrots in boiling, salted water 7–8 minutes; drain. Melt butter in saucepan, add carrots, and toss to coat on all sides. Stir in Mandarine Napoleon and cook 1 minute. Add cream and cook over low heat until cream coats carrots, about 5 minutes. Season to taste with salt and pepper.

4 servings

¾ pound carrots, sliced
1½ tablespoons butter
2 tablespoons Mandarine Napoleon
¼ cup cream
Salt
White pepper

POTATO-APPLE CASSEROLE

Combine water, sugar, 1 teaspoon salt, and pepper; bring to a boil. Add potatoes, apples, and mellow mash; bring back to a boil. Reduce heat, cover, and simmer until potatoes are tender; drain. Place mixture in casserole and season with remaining salt and pepper. Cook bacon until brown and crisp. Remove from skillet and reserve. Sauté onions in ¼ cup pan drippings until light brown. Stir reserved bacon into onions; pour contents of skillet over apple-potato mixture. Bake in preheated 350°F. oven 20 minutes. Serve with pork.

8 servings

2 cups cold water
1 tablespoon sugar
2 teaspoons salt
½ teaspoon black pepper
3 pounds potatoes, peeled and cut into 1-inch cubes
1 pound cooking apples, peeled, cored, and cut into 1½-inch-thick wedges
½ cup Yellowstone Mellow Mash
½ pound bacon, in ¼-inch cubes
2 onions, sliced and separated into rings

TANGY SWEET POTATO SOUFFLÉ

1 seventeen-ounce can
  sweet potatoes,
  drained and mashed
6 eggs, separated
1 cup milk
¼ cup Mandarine
  Napoleon
3 tablespoons brown
  sugar
½ teaspoon cinnamon
½ teaspoon salt
¼ cup finely chopped
  pecans

Combine sweet potatoes, egg yolks, milk, Mandarine Napoleon, sugar, cinnamon, and salt. Cook over medium heat, stirring constantly, until mixture comes to a boil. Cool slightly. Beat egg whites until stiff, but not dry, peaks form. Fold a third of the egg whites into sweet potato mixture. Fold in remaining egg whites. Spoon into 6-cup soufflé dish that has been buttered and sprinkled with half the nuts. Sprinkle remaining nuts over top. Bake in preheated 400°F. oven 20–25 minutes.

6–8 servings

ROTINI WITH APRICOT BRANDY SAUCE

3 small onions, chopped
¼ cup chopped parsley
1 clove garlic, minced
⅓ cup olive oil
1 sixteen-ounce can
  tomatoes, coarsely
  chopped
1 teaspoon sugar
½ teaspoon salt
½ cup Mr. Boston
  Apricot Flavored
  Brandy
12 black olives, chopped
1 pound rotini, cooked
  al dente
½ cup grated Parmesan
  cheese

Sauté onion, parsley, and garlic in oil until onions are soft. Add tomatoes, sugar, and salt; cook over low heat until sauce is thick. Stir in brandy and olives and simmer 10 minutes. Pour sauce over rotini, sprinkle with cheese, and toss to blend. Serve immediately.

6 servings

FUSILLI WITH WHISKEY CREAM SAUCE

Cook mushrooms, onion, parsley, and garlic in butter until tender. Add whiskey, salt, and pepper; reduce heat and simmer until most of liquid has evaporated, about 20 minutes. Add cream and fusilli; heat through. Sprinkle with cheese; toss lightly to blend. Serve with veal, poultry, or shellfish.

6–8 servings

½ cup sliced mushrooms
½ cup chopped onion
½ cup chopped parsley
1 clove garlic, minced
3 tablespoons butter
¾ cup Old Thompson American Whiskey
½ teaspoon salt
⅛ teaspoon pepper
1½ cups heavy cream
1 pound fusilli, cooked *al dente*
⅓ cup grated Parmesan cheese

FETTUCINI WITH ASPARAGUS

Beat eggs until smooth; add salt, pepper, and 2 tablespoons cheese; set aside. Melt butter; add ham and heat thoroughly. Add asparagus and anisette; simmer until liquid has almost evaporated, 5–8 minutes. Add fettucini, stir to blend, and heat thoroughly. Remove from heat, add egg mixture, and toss to blend. Sprinkle remaining cheese on top. Serve immediately.

6 servings

3 eggs
1 teaspoon salt
¼ teaspoon pepper
¾ cup grated Parmesan cheese
3 tablespoons butter
1 cup diced ham
½ pound fresh asparagus, cut into 1-inch pieces and cooked
¼ cup Mr. Boston Anisette
1 pound fettucini, cooked *al dente*

65

ALMOND-POPPY SEED NOODLES

1 cup sliced almonds
¼ cup poppy seeds
¾ cup butter
1 teaspoon salt
½ cup Amaretto di Saronno
1 pound egg noodles, cooked *al dente*

Cook almonds, salt, and poppy seeds in butter until almonds are golden brown. Add Amaretto di Saronno and cook until most of the liquid has evaporated, 5–6 minutes.

Pour almond-butter mixture over noodles. Toss and serve immediately with pork or chicken.

6–8 servings

CHEESEY RICE BAKE

1½ cups converted rice
1¾ cups chicken broth
1 cup Balfour Cream Sherry
1 cup water
½ cup Mr. Boston Anisette
1 sixteen-ounce can tomatoes
2 small zucchinis, sliced
2 small onions, sliced
½ cup butter
2 teaspoons salt
2 cloves garlic, minced
1 teaspoon basil
¼ teaspoon pepper
1 bay leaf
1 cup shredded Cheddar cheese
1 cup grated Romano cheese
1 cup heavy cream

Combine all ingredients except cheeses and cream in a 9 × 13-inch baking dish. Cover and bake in preheated 400°F. oven 30 minutes. Un-

cover and bake 30 minutes more. Stir in cheeses and cream. Bake, uncovered, 10 minutes longer.

8 servings

WILD SHERRY RICE

Bring water, 1 teaspoon salt, and 1 tablespoon butter to boil; stir in rice. Reduce heat to low and cook, covered, until water is absorbed and rice is tender, 45–50 minutes. Sauté pepper and onion in remaining ¼ cup butter 3 minutes. Add mushrooms, celery, sherry, remaining ¼ teaspoon salt, and pepper. Cook until most liquid has evaporated, 8–10 minutes. Mix with rice and heat through. Serve with pork, lamb, chicken, or duck.

4 servings

2½ cups water
1¼ teaspoons salt
¼ cup plus 1 tablespoon butter
1 six-ounce package wild rice
1 cup chopped sweet red pepper
¾ cup chopped onion
1 cup sliced mushrooms
¾ cup chopped celery
½ cup Balfour Cream Sherry
⅛ teaspoon pepper

BROCCOLI TIMBALES

Combine broccoli and eggs in blender or food processor and blend until smooth; set aside. Melt butter in saucepan and stir in flour until smooth; cook 1–2 minutes. Gradually add milk, stirring constantly, until smooth. Add seasonings and cook until thickened. Stir sauce and Mandarine Napoleon into broccoli purée. Pour into buttered timbale molds. Place molds in large pan with 2 inches of water. Bring to a boil on top of stove; cover loosely with aluminum foil and bake in preheated 350°F. oven 1½ hours or until set.

6–8 servings

2 cups chopped broccoli, cooked and drained
3 eggs
2 tablespoons butter
2 tablespoons flour
1 cup milk
½ teaspoon salt
⅛ teaspoon white pepper
⅛ teaspoon nutmeg
Cayenne pepper to taste
2 tablespoons Mandarine Napoleon

RED CABBAGE SAUTÉ WITH GIN

4 cups shredded red
   cabbage
2 tablespoons lard
2 teaspoons lemon juice
¼ teaspoon celery seed
⅛ teaspoon red pepper
   flakes
1 teaspoon salt
¼ teaspoon pepper
2 tablespoons Glenmore
   Gin
1 tablespoon chopped
   parsley

Cook red cabbage in lard and lemon juice over medium-high heat 2 minutes, stirring constantly. Add celery seed, red pepper, salt, and pepper; cook 2 minutes. Add gin and cook until liquid has evaporated, about 2 minutes. Stir in chopped parsley. Serve immediately.

4 servings

BRAISED CELERY HEARTS

2 pounds celery hearts,
   cut into 4-inch lengths
1 cup chicken broth
2 tablespoons Mr. Boston
   Anisette
2 tablespoons butter
Pepper
4 bacon slices

Remove strings from celery stalks; place in 1-quart ovenproof casserole. Combine chicken broth and anisette; pour over celery. Dot with butter and sprinkle with pepper. Place bacon slices over celery. Cover and bring to boil. Bake in preheated 350°F. oven 30 minutes. Remove bacon slices. Serve celery with juices.

4 servings

CORN AND OKRA FRITTERS

Combine corn, okra, green pepper, onion, pimiento, chili pepper, parsley, bourbon, eggs, and salt. Add biscuit mix a tablespoon at a time, mixing well after each addition. Let rest 5 minutes. Heat lard to 350°F.

Drop batter by rounded tablespoons into 2-inches hot, melted lard and fry to golden brown on each side; drain. Serve immediately.

6–8 servings

1 cup corn
½ cup sliced okra, blanched
¼ cup chopped green pepper
¼ cup chopped onion
2 teaspoons chopped pimiento
1 whole green chili pepper, chopped
2 tablespoons chopped parsley
2 tablespoons Old Kentucky Tavern Straight Bourbon Whiskey
2 eggs
½ teaspoon salt
5 tablespoons biscuit mix
Lard or shortening

MUSHROOM CREAM SHERRY SAUTÉ

Cook mushrooms in butter until golden brown. Stir in seasonings and sherry; cook 1 minute. Sprinkle with parsley. Serve immediately.

3–4 servings

½ pound mushrooms, sliced
2 tablespoons butter
½ teaspoon salt
¼ teaspoon white pepper
⅛ teaspoon nutmeg
¼ cup Balfour Cream Sherry
1 tablespoon chopped parsley

Salads and Dressings

Added to a salad of any one or an assortment of superior greens, crudités, crisp cooked vegetables, or fruits, the dressing provides the crowning touch. The exotic herbs and aromatics in liquors and liqueurs create slight shadings or even outright changes that improve the flavor of many dressings. A good general technique is to replace vinegars in whole or part with spirits, which themselves may be varied for new emphasis and enjoyment.

So, while we give you recipes for both salads and dressings as prototypes, we urge you to expand on the concept. Develop your own combinations of dressings and salad ingredients. Experiment—use your imagination.

FRUIT PLATTER CASSIS

Arrange fruits on platter; chill until ready to serve. Blend mayonnaise, sour cream, and crème de cassis until smooth. Serve over fresh fruit; garnish with mint.

6 servings

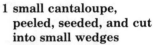

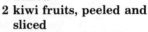

1 small cantaloupe, peeled, seeded, and cut into small wedges
1 pint strawberries, hulled
2 kiwi fruits, peeled and sliced
1 orange, peeled and sliced
½ pineapple, peeled, cored, and sliced
1 cup blueberries
⅓ cup mayonnaise
1 cup sour cream
⅓ cup Mr. Boston Crème de Cassis
Fresh mint

FANCIFUL FRUIT SALAD

Toss apple with lemon juice. Add grapes, celery, and walnuts. Blend mayonnaise and peach brandy. Pour over apple mixture; stir until fruits are coated. Chill at least 2 hours. Serve on a bed of lettuce leaves.

4 servings

2 cups coarsely chopped red apple
4 teaspoons lemon juice
1 cup seedless grapes
⅔ cup chopped celery
¾ cup broken walnuts
⅔ cup mayonnaise
2 tablespoons Mr. Boston Peach Flavored Brandy
Romaine lettuce leaves

73

CUCUMBER SALAD

1 cucumber, peeled and
  thinly sliced
1 teaspoon salt
1 tablespoon vinegar
1 tablespoon Glenmore
  Gin
2 tablespoons salad oil
½ teaspoon dried dill
  weed
¼ cup sour cream
⅛ teaspoon pepper
1 teaspoon sugar

Place cucumbers in colander and sprinkle with ½ teaspoon salt; let stand 20 minutes. Pat dry between paper towels. Combine vinegar, gin, oil, dill, sour cream, remaining ½ teaspoon salt, pepper, and sugar; blend well. Toss cucumber slices with dressing.

4 servings

MARINATED BRUSSELS SPROUTS

2 tablespoons red wine
  vinegar
3 tablespoons olive oil
3 tablespoons vegetable
  oil
1 tablespoon Glenmore
  Gin
½ teaspoon salt
¼ teaspoon pepper
½ teaspoon tarragon
2 cups brussels sprouts,
  cooked

Combine vinegar, oils, gin, and seasonings; blend thoroughly. Pour over brussels sprouts, cover, and refrigerate 3–5 hours.

4–6 servings

Fruit Platter Cassis

Spinach-Ricotta Torte

CAESAR SALAD

Combine egg, anchovy, vodka, lemon juice, garlic, mustard, and Worcestershire sauce; blend thoroughly. Pour over lettuce and toss.

Add olive oil, croutons, and cheese; toss to blend. Sprinkle with fresh ground pepper. Serve immediately.

2 servings

1 coddled egg (cooked 1 minute)
3 anchovy fillets, minced
1 tablespoon Glenmore Vodka
1 tablespoon lemon juice
1 clove garlic, minced
1 teaspoon prepared mustard
¼ teaspoon Worcestershire sauce
15 Romaine lettuce leaves, washed, dried, and torn in half
¼ cup olive oil
¼ cup croutons
3 tablespoons grated Parmesan cheese
Fresh ground black pepper

CURRIED AVOCADO SALAD

Blend mayonnaise, curry, and Mandarine Napoleon until smooth. Add avocado and chicken; stir to blend. Season to taste with salt and pepper. Serve on lettuce leaves and garnish with tomato wedges.

4 servings

½ cup mayonnaise
1 teaspoon curry powder
1 tablespoon Mandarine Napoleon
1 large avocado, diced
2 cups cooked, diced chicken
Salt
Pepper
Lettuce leaves
Tomato wedges

WILTED SPINACH SALAD

½ cup chopped green
  onion
¼ cup white wine
  vinegar
2 tablespoons Mr.
  Boston Anisette
1 tablespoon prepared
  mustard
⅛ teaspoon fresh ground
  pepper
5 slices bacon, cooked
  crisp and crumbled;
  reserve ¼ cup
  drippings
1 pound spinach leaves,
  cleaned and stemmed

Cook onions, vinegar, anisette, mustard, and pepper in reserved bacon drippings just until thoroughly heated. Pour over spinach and toss. Sprinkle with crumbled bacon. Serve immediately.

3–4 servings

DEVONSHIRE POTATO SALAD

10 potatoes, peeled,
  sliced, and cooked
1 cup chopped onion
1 cup chopped celery
2 scallions, chopped
¼ cup chopped parsley
1 clove garlic, minced
½ cup mayonnaise
⅓ cup Glenmore Gin
¼ cup olive oil
1 tablespoon Dijon
  mustard
1 teaspoon salt
½ teaspoon pepper

Combine vegetables. Blend remaining ingredients, mixing well. Pour over vegetables and stir lightly. Serve hot or cold.

6–8 servings

ORANGE AND ONION SALAD

Layer watercress, orange sections, and onion rings. Combine remaining ingredients and blend thoroughly. Pour over salad and sprinkle with pepper just before serving.

4–6 servings

1 bunch watercress leaves
4 oranges, peeled, sectioned
1 red onion, sliced, separated into rings
2 tablespoons honey
1 tablespoon vinegar
2 tablespoons Mr. Boston Crème de Cassis
1 tablespoon lemon juice
¼ cup salad oil
¼ teaspoon celery seed
¼ teaspoon salt
Fresh ground pepper

TOMATO SALAD WITH COGNAC CREAM DRESSING

½ cup sour cream
¼ cup heavy cream
2 tablespoons catsup
2 tablespoons Rémy Martin V.S.O.P. Cognac
2 tablespoons minced parsley
1 teaspoon tarragon
½ teaspoon salt
⅛ teaspoon white pepper
1–1½ pounds ripe tomatoes, peeled and sliced
2–3 green onions, chopped
½ cup sliced, pitted black olives

Combine sour cream, cream, catsup, cognac, parsley, and seasonings; stir to blend. Sprinkle tomatoes with onions and olives.

Pour dressing over top.

6–8 servings

Note: Cognac Cream also may be used as a dip for boiled or steamed shrimp and crudités.

ORIENTAL DRESSING

⅓ cup vinegar
¼ cup peanut oil
2 tablespoons Mr. Boston Ginger Flavored Brandy
1 tablespoon soy sauce
1 tablespoon peanut butter, smooth
2 teaspoons sugar

Combine all ingredients in blender and blend until smooth. Serve over tossed green or pasta salad.

Makes 1 cup

GREEN GODDESS DRESSING

Place all ingredients in blender and blend until smooth. Chill. Serve over tossed green salad.

Makes 1¾ cups

1 cup mayonnaise
½ cup sour cream
¼ cup minced parsley
3 anchovy fillets, minced
2 tablespoons minced green onion
1 tablespoon Mr. Boston Anisette
1 tablespoon lemon juice
¼ teaspoon tarragon
1 clove garlic, minced
½ teaspoon salt
⅛ teaspoon pepper

SWEET AND TANGY DRESSING

Blend all ingredients until smooth. Chill. Serve over fresh fruit.

Makes 1⅓ cups

1 cup mayonnaise
¼ cup Mandarine Napoleon
2 tablespoons honey

CHUTNEY DRESSING

Blend all ingredients until thoroughly mixed. Chill. Serve on chicken salads and fruit salads.

Makes 1 cup

½ cup olive oil
3 tablespoons Mr. Boston Apricot Flavored Brandy
3 tablespoons half-and-half or light cream
2 tablespoons chutney
2 tablespoons lime juice
1 teaspoon sugar
¼ teaspoon curry powder
⅛ teaspoon salt
⅛ teaspoon white pepper

CREAMY BLEU CHEESE DRESSING

½ cup mayonnaise
¼ cup crumbled bleu
   cheese
4 anchovy fillets, rinsed
   and minced
2 tablespoons olive oil
2 tablespoons Mr.
   Boston Five Star
   Brandy
2 teaspoons prepared
   mustard

Blend all ingredients until thoroughly mixed. Chill. Serve on tossed salads, potatoes, or as a dip for crudités.

Makes 1⅓ cups

CAVIAR DRESSING

1 cup sour cream
2 ounces red caviar
2 tablespoons minced
   onion
2 tablespoons Glenmore
   Vodka
1 tablespoon lemon juice

Blend all ingredients until smooth. Chill. Serve on cucumbers, boiled new potatoes, hard-cooked eggs, or cold poached salmon.

Makes 1½ cups

Lunch/Brunch

Brunch—as an easy way to entertain or as a weekend or holiday meal—has become a tradition. This book and its step-by-step instructions on the use of spirits in food preparation and cooking can make the tradition even more fun. New dishes are given a spirited zest that makes them festive. And no matter how much you like an old favorite, you will find that the prudent addition of spirits makes it even better. Tequila makes Mexican Egg Pie special; a banana pancake with crème de banana is a tropical treat.

Many of the simpler items included among appetizers and side dishes also lend themselves to lunch or brunch. Use the menu guide and liquor index as an idea file to supplement the offerings in this section.

PAPAYA PINEAPPLE COMPOTE

Combine fruits, papaya nectar, Mandarine Napoleon, and spices; stir to blend. Pour into 2-quart baking dish and dot with butter. Bake in preheated 350°F. oven 20 minutes. Serve hot, topped with sour cream.

6 servings

2 cups pineapple chunks
1 eleven-ounce can mandarin orange sections, drained
1 cup seedless grapes
1 cup strawberries
¾ cup papaya nectar
¼ cup Mandarine Napoleon
¼ teaspoon cloves
¼ teaspoon nutmeg
¼ teaspoon cinnamon
2 tablespoons butter
Sour cream

EGGS FLORENTINE

Place half of the spinach in greased shallow 1½-quart baking dish. Sprinkle with nutmeg and Swiss cheese. Top with remaining spinach. Melt 2 tablespoons butter in saucepan; blend in flour, salt, and pepper. Heat until bubbly. Gradually add milk and cream sherry, stirring until blended. Cook 1–2 minutes. Remove from heat. Fry eggs in remaining 1 tablespoon butter, covered, over low heat, about 2 minutes. Arrange eggs on top of spinach. Spoon sauce over eggs. Sprinkle with Cheddar cheese. Bake in preheated 325°F. oven 15 minutes. Serve immediately.

4 servings

2 ten-ounce packages frozen chopped spinach, cooked and drained
Dash nutmeg
½ cup shredded Swiss cheese
3 tablespoons butter
2 tablespoons flour
1 teaspoon salt
¼ teaspoon white pepper
1⅓ cups milk
¼ cup Balfour Cream Sherry
4 eggs
¼ cup shredded Cheddar cheese

❦❦❦❦❦
ASTI FRUIT BOWL

6 cups mixed fresh fruit
  chunks*
1 cup Torre Dei Conti
  Asti Spumante
¼ teaspoon ground
  coriander

Combine all ingredients, blending
well. Serve immediately.

6 servings

*Suggested fruits: melons, grapes, berries,
peaches, pears, apples, pineapple, oranges,
and grapefruit

❦❦❦❦❦
PORK SAUSAGE HASH WITH POACHED EGGS

¾ pound bulk pork
  sausage
¾ cup chopped onion
⅓ cup chopped celery
1½ cups diced, cooked
  potatoes
⅓ cup Mr. Boston Five
  Star Brandy
3 tablespoons minced
  parsley
1 teaspoon
  Worcestershire sauce
¼ teaspoon caraway
  seeds
¼ teaspoon salt
⅛ teaspoon pepper
6 poached eggs

Brown sausage; add onion and celery and cook until vegetables are
tender, about 5 minutes. Add potatoes, brandy, parsley, Worcestershire sauce, caraway seeds, salt,
and pepper. Cook over medium
heat until liquid has evaporated.
Serve poached eggs over hash.

6 servings

SHERRIED EGGS IN POTATO SKINS

Melt 2 tablespoons butter in saucepan. Stir in flour and cook until bubbly. Remove from heat; blend in sour cream and cream sherry, return to heat, and cook until bubbly and smooth. Set aside. Beat eggs with salt and pepper. Melt remaining 2 tablespoons butter, add eggs, and cook until eggs are softly set. Remove from heat. Gently stir in sour cream mixture. Spoon filling into Potato Skins and sprinkle with bacon, cheese, and chives. Broil until cheese bubbles and begins to brown.

6 servings

4 tablespoons butter
2 tablespoons flour
1 cup sour cream
½ cup Balfour Cream Sherry
12 eggs
¾ teaspoon salt
⅛ teaspoon white pepper
½ pound bacon, cooked crisp and crumbled
1 cup shredded Cheddar cheese
½ cup chopped chives
Potato Skins (see below)

Potato Skins

Rub potatoes with 2 tablespoons butter. Prick each potato with fork and bake in preheated 425°F. oven 1 hour. Cut potatoes in half, lengthwise. Scoop out pulp and reserve for other use. Place shells on baking sheet. Melt remaining 6 tablespoons butter and brush inside of each potato. Sprinkle with salt and pepper. Return to oven and bake 20–30 minutes.

6 baking potatoes, scrubbed
½ cup butter
Salt
Pepper

MEXICAN EGG PIE

½ pound hot Italian
   sausage
⅔ cup chopped onion
⅔ cup chopped red or
   green pepper
2 ten-inch wheat tortillas
1 sixteen-ounce can
   refried beans
¼ cup shredded Cheddar
   cheese
¼ cup shredded
   Monterey Jack cheese
⅔ cup sour cream
8 eggs
¼ cup Gavilan Tequila
¾ teaspoon salt
⅛ teaspoon cayenne
   pepper

Remove sausage from casing and brown in skillet; remove from skillet and drain on paper towels. Cook onion and pepper in sausage drippings 5–6 minutes. Place tortillas in two greased 8- or 9-inch pie pans. Spread half the beans over each tortilla. Top each with a layer of sausage. Add half the peppers and onions to each pie. Sprinkle with cheeses. Beat together eggs, sour cream, tequila, salt, and cayenne until smooth. Pour half the egg mixture into each pie shell. Bake in preheated 300°F. oven 30 minutes or until knife inserted near center comes out clean.

8–10 servings

SWEET AND SAVORY CANADIAN BACON

1 cup brown sugar,
   packed
6 tablespoons
   Mandarine Napoleon
¼ cup red wine vinegar
¼ cup Dijon mustard
1 tablespoon soy sauce
2 teaspoons prepared
   horseradish
1 ten-inch square frozen
   puff pastry
2 pounds Canadian
   bacon
1 egg
1 tablespoon water

Heat sugar, Mandarine Napoleon, vinegar, mustard, soy sauce, and horseradish until sugar is dissolved. Roll out puff pastry until large enough to enclose bacon. Brush bacon and pastry with sauce. Roll bacon in pastry, brushed side in, pinching to seal edges. Beat egg and water until smooth; brush over pastry. Place bacon in greased baking dish. Bake in preheated 425°F. oven 25–30 minutes or until pastry is golden brown. Serve bacon with remaining sauce.

6–8 servings

SPINACH-RICOTTA TORTE

Stir together flour and ½ teaspoon salt. Cut in butter until mixture resembles coarse crumbs. Mix in water, 1–2 tablespoons at a time, until crumbs form ball. Cover and refrigerate 1 hour. Cook onion in olive oil 3 minutes. Stir in spinach and cook 5 minutes. Add anisette and marjoram and cook until liquid has evaporated, about 5 minutes. Remove from heat and blend in 2 eggs, ½ teaspoon salt, and ⅛ teaspoon pepper. Cook sausage until browned. Drain and crumble. Blend ricotta cheese, cream, rosemary, and remaining ¼ teaspoon salt and ⅛ tea-spoon pepper. On lightly floured surface, roll out dough to a 16-inch circle ⅛-inch thick. Place in lightly greased 1-quart soufflé dish, allowing pastry to hang over sides. Layer into pastry half the spinach, half the sausage, all the ricotta mixture, remaining sausage, and remaining spinach. Bring pastry up to cover mixture; trim so that pastry overlaps only once and cut small hole in center. Beat remaining egg and brush over pastry. Bake in preheated 375°F. oven 1 hour or until lightly browned.

6–8 servings

2 cups flour
1¼ teaspoons salt
¾ cup butter
⅓–½ cup ice water
½ cup onion
3 tablespoons olive oil
2 ten-ounce packages frozen, chopped spinach, thawed and well drained
¼ cup Mr. Boston Anisette
½ teaspoon marjoram
3 eggs, beaten
¼ teaspoon pepper
¾ pound mild Italian sausage
1 cup ricotta cheese
¼ cup cream
¼ teaspoon rosemary

ASPARAGUS PROSCIUTTO BAKE

¼ pound thinly sliced prosciutto*
6 slices mozzarella cheese
1 pound asparagus spears, cooked
2 tablespoons butter
1 tablespoon flour
½ cup half-and-half
¼ cup Balfour Cream Sherry
1 tablespoon Dijon mustard
¼ teaspoon salt
⅛ teaspoon white pepper
Grated Parmesan cheese

Separate prosciutto slices; top each with cheese slice. Place 2–3 asparagus spears (depending on size) in center of each. Fold ends over asparagus; place on lightly greased baking sheet. Melt butter in saucepan, blend in flour, and cook over medium heat 2 minutes. Gradually add half-and-half and cook until thickened, stirring constantly. Add sherry, mustard, salt, and pepper; cook another 2–3 minutes. Pour over ham rolls, sprinkle with Parmesan cheese, and broil until sauce is hot and bubbly, 5–6 minutes.

6 servings

*Peppered ham may be substituted.

STRAWBERRY OMELETTE

1 ten-ounce package frozen, sliced strawberries in syrup, thawed
¼ cup butter
¼ cup Mandarine Napoleon
¼ cup sour cream
8 eggs
½ teaspoon salt
8–10 whole fresh strawberries, sliced

Combine fruit in syrup, 2 tablespoons butter, and 2 tablespoons Mandarine Napoleon in saucepan; bring to a boil. Cook over medium heat, stirring occasionally, until mixture is slightly thickened, 10–15 minutes. Remove from heat, stir in sour cream, and cover to keep warm. Beat eggs, salt, and remaining 2 tablespoons Mandarine Napoleon. Melt remaining 2 tablespoons butter over medium heat, add half the egg mixture, and scramble lightly until eggs begin to set. Place half the fresh sliced strawberries along center of omelette; fold omelette over strawberries and cook 30–40 seconds more. Divide into 2 servings. Spoon berry sauce over top. Repeat with remaining egg mixture.

3–4 servings

PUFFY BANANA PANCAKE

Place eggs, milk, crème de banana, flour, and salt in blender jar; blend until smooth. Melt 1 tablespoon butter in each of two 8-inch round baking pans. Add half the batter to each pan. Spoon banana slices evenly over batter. Bake in preheated 425°F. oven 15–18 minutes or until puffed and golden. Sprinkle with confectioners' sugar.

2–4 servings

4 eggs
½ cup milk
⅓ cup Mr. Boston Crème de Banana
¼ cup flour
¼ teaspoon salt
2 tablespoons butter
1 small banana, thinly sliced
Confectioners' sugar

PEACHY FRENCH TOAST WITH SAUSAGE

Blend eggs, yogurt, 2 tablespoons brandy, and allspice until smooth. Soak bread in mixture 5 minutes. Cook sausage links until browned; remove from skillet, drain, and keep warm. Drain fat from skillet; add remaining 2 tablespoons brandy and cook over medium-high meat, stirring constantly, about 2 minutes. Add 2 tablespoons butter and brown sugar to pan drippings; reduce to medium heat, cook and stir until sugar melts. Add peaches and cook until thoroughly heated. Return sausage to skillet and simmer until done, 5–8 minutes. In separate skillet, cook French bread slices in remaining 3 tablespoons butter and oil until golden brown on both sides. Serve with fruited sausage.

6 servings

6 eggs
½ cup yogurt
¼ cup Mr. Boston Peach Flavored Brandy
¼ teaspoon allspice
12 diagonal cut slices French bread
1 pound pork sausage links
5 tablespoons butter
3 tablespoons brown sugar
1 twenty-six-ounce can peach halves, drained
1 tablespoon oil

RICE CAKES

3 cups milk
½ cup uncooked rice
¼ teaspoon salt
⅓ cup sugar
4 tablespoons butter
1 tablespoon grated orange peel
3 tablespoons Mr. Boston Virgin Islands Dark Rum
2 eggs, separated

Heat milk to boiling; add rice and salt, reduce heat, cover, and simmer 15 minutes. Stir in sugar, butter, orange peel, and rum and cook 15 minutes more or until rice is tender. Remove from heat; blend in egg yolks. Beat egg whites until stiff; fold into rice mixture and divide among 10 buttered and sugared 6-ounce custard cups. Bake in preheated 375°F. oven 25–30 minutes. Serve with ham or Canadian bacon.

6–8 servings

SHRIMP AND EGGS ROYALE

1 cup sliced mushrooms
¼ cup butter
6 tablespoons Balfour Cream Sherry
1 8-ounce package frozen medium shrimp
1 13-ounce can shrimp bisque
1 10-ounce package frozen chopped spinach, cooked and drained
¼ teaspoon salt
¼ teaspoon pepper
12 eggs
6 English muffins, split

Cook mushrooms in butter and 2 tablespoons sherry until tender. Add shrimp and cook until thawed; set aside. Combine ¾ cup shrimp bisque, spinach, and ⅛ teaspoon each of salt and pepper; heat thoroughly. Combine remaining bisque, cream sherry, and ⅛ teaspoon each of salt and pepper and simmer 5 minutes. Poach eggs. Toast English muffin halves. Layer about 1 tablespoon spinach mixture, 1 tablespoon shrimp-mushroom mixture, and egg on each muffin half. Top with cream sherry-bisque mixture. Serve immediately.

6 servings

Shrimp and Eggs Royale

Breads

90

CRAB AND GRAPEFRUIT SALAD

Combine whipped cream, tequila, horseradish, lime juice, salt, and pepper; stir to blend. Pour over crabmeat; toss lightly until crabmeat is evenly coated. Line serving platter with lettuce leaves, place crab mixture in center, and surround with grapefruit sections. Sprinkle parsley over top.

6–8 servings

2 cups heavy cream, whipped
¼ cup Gavilan Tequila
3 tablespoons prepared horseradish
1½ tablespoons lime juice
¼ teaspoon salt
¼ teaspoon white pepper
4 cups chunked Alaskan king crabmeat
Lettuce leaves
3 pink grapefruits, peeled and sectioned
¼ cup chopped parsley

SALMON-STUFFED TOMATOES

Cut tops off tomatoes; scoop out insides; remove seeds. Chop pulp and reserve. Sprinkle insides with wine vinegar and drain. Sauté green onions and tomato pulp in butter 1 minute. Add cognac and cook until liquid has almost evaporated, 5–6 minutes. Blend cream cheese, salmon, and pepper; stir in onion-tomato mixture. Spoon into tomatoes and bake in preheated 425°F. oven 10–15 minutes or until stuffing begins to brown. Serve hot.

4 servings

4 medium tomatoes
2 tablespoons wine vinegar
2 tablespoons butter
½ cup chopped green onion
½ cup Rémy Martin V.S.O.P. Cognac
2 three-ounce packages cream cheese
5 ounces smoked salmon, chopped
¼ teaspoon black pepper

HANGTOWN FRY

3 bacon slices, cut into
   1-inch pieces
1 eight-ounce can
   oysters, drained;
   reserve liquid
3 tablespoons flour
1 tablespoon butter
4 eggs
1 tablespoon Mr. Boston
   Anisette
⅛ teaspoon salt
Dash pepper
1 tablespoon chopped
   parsley
¼ cup lemon juice

Fry bacon until crisp and drain on paper towels. Dust the oysters with the flour, shaking off excess. Brown in butter and bacon drippings on both sides; remove from skillet and set aside. Beat together eggs, anisette, 1 tablespoon reserved oyster liquid, salt, and pepper. Cook, stirring constantly, until eggs are softly set. Spread eggs evenly over skillet; top with oysters, bacon, and parsley and sprinkle with lemon juice. Cook until bottom browns and eggs are set. Cut into quarters to serve.

4 servings

Breads

How can you make more of bread than to simply call it by its familiar accolade—"the staff of life"? You can improve its flavor, give it distinction and mystery with the addition of spirits. To pumpernickel, add bourbon; to blueberry muffins, add Triple Sec; to bacon biscuits, add brandy.

How can you make more of a meal that consists only of a salad or soup? Serve spirited bread. And a brown-bagged ham-on-rye sandwich becomes a gourmet luncheon when the bread is Orange Rye Bread flavored with Triple Sec.

SWISS CHEESE AND MUSTARD BREAD

Stir together 2 cups flour and yeast. Heat together milk, ¼ cup brandy, oil, sugar, mustard, and salt until very warm to touch (120°F.); blend into flour mixture and beat until smooth. Blend in eggs and cheese. Add enough additional flour to make a moderately stiff dough. Knead on lightly floured surface until smooth and satiny, 8–10 minutes. Cover dough with bowl or pan and let stand 30 minutes. Divide dough in half.

Shape each half into ball and place in greased 1½-quart round baking dish, turning to grease all sides. Let rise in a warm place (80–85°F.) until doubled, about 1 hour. Bake in preheated 375°F. oven 25–30 minutes, or until loaf makes hollow sound when thumped. Combine butter and remaining 1 tablespoon brandy and brush over loaves. Cool on wire rack.

2 loaves

5½–6 cups flour
2 packages dry yeast
¾ cup milk
¼ cup plus 1 tablespoon Mr. Boston Apple-Flavored Brandy
¼ cup oil
2 tablespoons sugar
2 tablespoons Dijon mustard
2 teaspoons salt
3 eggs at room temperature, lightly beaten
2 cups shredded Swiss cheese
2 tablespoons butter, melted

PUMPERNICKEL BREAD

2 cups rye flour
1½–2 cups all-purpose
   flour
2 packages dry yeast
1 cup milk
1 cup water
¼ cup Yellowstone
   Straight Bourbon
   Whiskey
¼ cup margarine
¼ cup molasses
1 tablespoon instant
   coffee
1 tablespoon cocoa
1 tablespoon salt
1 egg
2 cups whole wheat
   flour

Stir together 1 cup rye flour, 1 cup all-purpose flour and yeast. Heat milk, water, bourbon, margarine, molasses, coffee, cocoa, and salt until very warm to touch (120°F.); blend into flour mixture and beat until smooth. Beat in egg. Add remaining rye flour, whole wheat flour, and enough all-purpose flour to make moderately stiff dough. Knead on lightly floured surface until smooth and satiny, 8–10 minutes. Place dough in greased bowl, turning to grease all sides. Cover and let rise in a warm place until doubled, 1½–2 hours. Punch down; let rest 10 minutes. Divide dough in half and shape each half into round loaf. Place on greased baking sheet in a warm place and let rise until doubled, about 1 hour. Bake in preheated 375°F. oven 30–40 minutes or until loaf makes hollow sound when thumped.

2 loaves

ORANGE RYE BREAD

Stir together 1 cup rye flour, 1 cup all-purpose flour, and yeast. Heat liquid ingredients with sugar, salt, and orange peel until very warm to touch (120°F.); blend into flour mixture and beat until smooth. Add remaining rye flour and enough all-purpose flour to make moderately stiff dough. Let rest 10 minutes. Knead on lightly floured surface until smooth and satiny, about 10 minutes. Place in greased bowl, turning to grease all sides. Cover and let rise in warm place until doubled, 60–75 minutes. Punch down. Divide dough in half. Shape each half into loaf. Place on greased baking sheet, brush with oil, and let rise until doubled, 50–60 minutes. Bake in preheated 375°F. oven 30–40 minutes, or until loaf sounds hollow when thumped.

2 loaves

3 cups rye flour
3–3½ cups all-purpose flour
2 packages dry yeast
1 cup water
1 cup milk
¼ cup oil
¼ cup **Mr. Boston Triple Sec**
2 tablespoons brown sugar
1 tablespoon salt
1 tablespoon grated orange peel

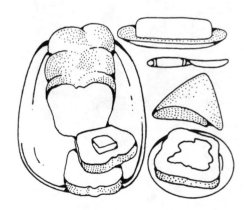

ANISE ROLLS

4½–5 cups flour
 2 packages dry yeast
½ cup milk
½ cup sugar
¼ cup water
¼ cup Mr. Boston
   Anisette
¼ cup oil
 2 teaspoons anise seed
 2 teaspoons salt
 2 eggs at room
   temperature
Oil

Stir together 2 cups flour and yeast. Heat milk, sugar, water, anisette, ¼ cup oil, anise seed, and salt over low heat until very warm to touch (120°F.); blend into flour mixture and beat until smooth. Blend in eggs. Add 1 cup flour and beat until smooth. Stir in enough additional flour to make a moderately stiff dough. Turn onto lightly floured surface and knead until smooth and satiny, 8–10 minutes. Shape into ball and place in lightly greased bowl, turning to grease all sides. Cover and let rise in a warm place (80–85°F.) until doubled, about 1½ hours. Punch down. Divide in half; let rest 10 minutes. Divide each half into 12 equal pieces. Shape each piece into 16-inch-long rope. Shape each rope into a bow; place on greased baking sheets. Brush with oil. Let rise in a warm place until doubled, about 30 minutes. Bake in preheated 350°F. oven 20–25 minutes, or until rolls are golden brown.

24 rolls

ITALIAN SWEET BREAD

Stir together 2 cups flour, yeast, and 1 teaspoon salt. Heat 1 cup milk until very warm to touch (120°F.); blend into flour mixture until smooth. Cover and let stand in warm place until doubled in bulk, 1–1½ hours. Heat remaining milk; pour over raisins and let stand 20–30 minutes. Stir down batter; add raisin mixture, sugar, butter, eggs, rum, anisette, orange peel, and remaining 1 teaspoon salt; beat until smooth. Stir in enough additional flour to make moderately stiff dough. Turn onto lightly floured surface and knead until smooth and satiny, 10–15 minutes. Shape into 2 round loaves and place on greased baking sheet. Cover and let rise in warm place until doubled in bulk, 1–1½ hours. Bake in preheated 350°F. oven 60–70 minutes or until loaf sounds hollow when thumped. Cool completely on wire rack before slicing.

2 loaves

7½–8 cups flour
2 packages dry yeast
2 teaspoons salt
2 cups milk
1 cup raisins
1 cup sugar
½ cup butter, melted
4 eggs, room temperature
¼ cup Mr. Boston Virgin Islands Light Rum
¼ cup Mr. Boston Anisette
1 teaspoon dried grated orange peel

BLUEBERRY MUFFINS

Combine blueberries and Triple Sec; let stand 20 minutes. Stir together flour, sugar, baking powder, salt, and spices. Blend milk, oil, and egg until smooth. Add liquid and blueberry mixture all at once to flour, stirring only until flour is moistened. Pour batter into greased or paper-lined muffin cups. Bake in preheated 400°F. oven 25–30 minutes or until golden brown.

16–18 muffins

1 cup blueberries
¼ cup Mr. Boston Triple Sec
2 cups flour
½ cup sugar
2 teaspoons baking powder
1 teaspoon salt
½ teaspoon cinnamon
½ teaspoon nutmeg
1 cup milk
½ cup oil
1 egg, beaten

BLOODY MARY MUFFINS

2 cups flour
1 tablespoon baking powder
1 teaspoon salt
½ cup tomato juice
⅓ cup oil
¼ cup Glenmore Vodka
1½ teaspoons Worcestershire sauce
¼ teaspoon hot pepper sauce
2 eggs, beaten
¼ cup chopped celery

Stir together flour, baking powder, and salt. Blend tomato juice, oil, vodka, Worcestershire sauce, hot pepper sauce, and eggs until smooth. Blend into flour mixture just until moistened. Stir in celery. Pour into greased or paper-lined muffin cups. Bake in preheated 375°F. oven 20–25 minutes.

12 muffins

BRANDY BACON BISCUITS

2 cups flour
1 tablespoon baking powder
1 teaspoon salt
¼ cup cooked, crumbled bacon
3 tablespoons chopped chives
¼ cup shortening
1 cup sour cream
¼ cup Mr. Boston Five Star Brandy

Stir together flour, baking powder, salt, bacon, and chives. Cut in shortening until mixture resembles coarse crumbs. Blend sour cream and brandy. Stir into flour just until dough forms ball. Knead gently on lightly floured surface 30 seconds. Roll to ½-inch thickness and cut with floured 2-inch biscuit cutter. Place on greased baking sheet. Bake in preheated 400°F. oven 12–15 minutes or until golden brown.

15–18 biscuits

SWISS WHEAT BREAD

Stir together flours, cheese, sugar, baking powder, salt, and soda. Combine milk, oil, brandy, and eggs; blend until smooth. Add liquid mixture all at once to flour mixture, stirring only until flour is moistened. Pour into greased 8½ × 4½-inch loaf pan. Bake in preheated 375°F. oven 55–65 minutes or until cake tester comes out clean. Cool 10 minutes before removing from pan.

1 loaf

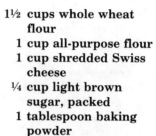

1½ cups whole wheat flour
1 cup all-purpose flour
1 cup shredded Swiss cheese
¼ cup light brown sugar, packed
1 tablespoon baking powder
1½ teaspoons salt
1 teaspoon baking soda
1¼ cups milk
⅓ cup oil
¼ cup Mr. Boston Apricot Flavored Brandy
2 eggs, beaten

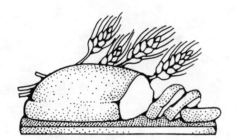

OLIVE CHEESE BREAD

2½ cups flour
1 cup shredded
   Cheddar cheese
½ cup chopped stuffed
   green olives
3 tablespoons sugar
4 teaspoons baking
   powder
1 teaspoon salt
¾ cup milk
⅓ cup oil
¼ cup Glenmore Gin
3 eggs, beaten

Stir together flour, cheese, olives, sugar, baking powder, and salt. Combine milk, oil, gin, and eggs; blend until smooth. Add to flour mixture, stirring only until flour is moistened. Pour into greased 8½ × 4½-inch loaf pan. Bake in preheated 350°F. oven 60–70 minutes or until cake tester comes out clean. Cover with foil, if necessary, to prevent excessive browning. Let stand 10 minutes before removing from pan.

1 loaf

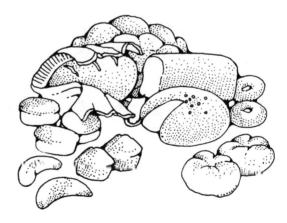

Desserts and Beverages

Nowhere has the use of cordials and spirits in cooking achieved such popular acceptance as in desserts and beverages.

Desserts, toppings, frostings, fillings, and sauces—all are receptive to the magic of liquor and liqueurs. The addition of spirits gives each dessert a new essence and makes it better. In fact, there are so many dessert recipes that we needed a separate companion volume to cover the variety adequately. We have compiled an entire range of them in the **Mr. Boston Spirited Dessert Guide,** but here are a few especially created for this concluding section.

Of course, spirits have always been part of the beverage list, alone or in combination with other ingredients. The beverages presented here were chosen as exceptional—new, different, and representing the last word in memorable food experiences.

APRICOTS ALLA AMARETTO

Bring apricot syrup to a boil, reduce heat, and simmer 15–20 minutes, or until syrup is thickened. Add Amaretto di Saronno and boil 5 minutes more. Pour over apricots, cover, and refrigerate several hours. Top with dollop of whipped cream and almonds before serving.

4–6 servings

1 nineteen-ounce can whole, unpeeled apricots, drained; reserve syrup
⅓ cup Amaretto di Saronno
Sweetened whipped cream
Slivered toasted almonds

RUM RAISIN BAKED APPLES

Place apples in 2-quart casserole. Stir together sugar, raisins, and almonds. Fill apple centers with mixture. Pour rum mixed with melted butter over apples. Cover and bake in preheated 350°F. oven 35–45 minutes or until apples are tender. Serve warm, with cream if desired.

6 large, red baking apples, cored
¼ cup brown sugar, packed
¼ cup raisins
¼ cup slivered almonds
½ cup Mr. Boston Virgin Islands Dark Rum
2 tablespoons butter, melted

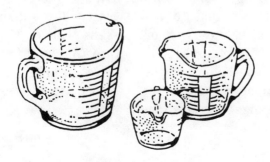

STRAWBERRIES IN ALMOND CREAM

1 quart fresh
  strawberries, cleaned
  and hulled
⅓ cup sugar
2 tablespoons Amaretto
  di Saronno
½ cup heavy cream

Sprinkle strawberries with sugar and let stand 1 hour. Drain and slice strawberries, reserving syrup. Set aside. Blend reserved syrup and Amaretto di Saronno. Whip cream until stiff. Blend in Amaretto di Saronno mixture and beat until stiff. Just before serving, fold sliced strawberries into almond cream.

6 servings

FROSTED ORANGES SARONNO

2 cups water
1¼ cups sugar
¼ cup lemon juice
1 tablespoon grated
  lemon peel
¾ cup Amaretto di
  Saronno
3 egg whites
6 large oranges
2 tablespoons minced
  coconut
½ cup chopped
  cranberries

Bring water and ¾ cup sugar to a boil; boil 5 minutes. Remove from heat and stir in lemon juice and peel and ½ cup Amaretto di Saronno. Freeze until mushy, 4–5 hours. Remove from freezer and beat until smooth. Beat 2 egg whites until stiff, fold into frozen mixture, and freeze until firm. Cut tops off oranges and remove pulp, keeping skin and as much of the pulp as possible intact. Remove strings and seeds from orange sections and combine sections with ¼ cup Amaretto di Saronno, cranberries, and coconut; chill. Beat remaining egg white until foamy; brush over orange lids and shells. Roll shells and lids in remaining ½ cup sugar; let stand at room temperature until crusty, 45–60 minutes. Fill orange shells with orange-cranberry mixture. Top with frozen mixture. Replace orange tops and serve immediately

6 servings

Traditional Strawberry Shortcake
Italian Love Cake

BAKED PEARS WITH GINGER CARAMEL

Place pear halves flat side down in a casserole dish. Combine brown sugar, brandy, and butter; cook over medium heat until sugar dissolves, 3–5 minutes. Pour liquid over pear halves and bake in preheated 350°F. oven 20–25 minutes. Increase heat to 400°F. Stir cream into pan liquid, baste pears with sauce, and bake about 10 minutes longer, or until pears are tender and sauce is slightly thickened. Serve sauce over pears. Top with whipped cream, if desired.

4 servings

4 pears, peeled, cored, and halved
¼ cup brown sugar, packed
¼ cup Mr. Boston Ginger Flavored Brandy
2 tablespoons butter
¼ cup cream

MOCHA CHIP MOUSSE

Sprinkle gelatin over water. Let stand 5 minutes. Heat until gelatin dissolves; stir in ¾ cup chocolate chips and ¼ cup brandy. Continue cooking, stirring constantly, until chocolate melts. Remove from heat and cool to room temperature. Beat egg yolks and remaining ¼ cup brandy until foamy. Add 2 tablespoons sugar and beat until thick, about 5 minutes. Gradually beat in chocolate mixture. Beat egg whites until foamy. Gradually add remaining ¼ cup sugar to egg whites and continue beating until stiff, but not dry, peaks form. Fold chocolate mixture into egg whites. Gently fold in whipped cream and remaining chocolate chips. Spoon into 1½-quart soufflé dish. Chill until set, 3–4 hours.

6 servings

1 tablespoon unflavored gelatin
¼ cup water
1¼ cups mini semi-sweet chocolate chips
½ cup Mr. Boston Coffee Flavored Brandy
5 eggs, separated
6 tablespoons sugar
1 cup heavy cream, whipped.

MOCHA POTS DE CRÈME

3 cups heavy cream
9 egg yolks
⅓ cup sugar
Dash salt
2 tablespoons Mr.
  Boston Coffee
  Flavored Brandy
1 tablespoon Rémy
  Martin V.S.O.P.
  Cognac

Beat together cream, egg yolks, sugar, salt, brandy, and cognac until well blended. Pour into 12 individual "pots" or ovenproof dishes. Place in a shallow baking pan with 1 inch hot water in the bottom. Bake in preheated 325°F. oven 30–35 minutes, or until knife inserted near center comes out clean. Serve at room temperature in individual pots.

12 servings

ALMOND ORANGE SOUFFLÉ

8 eggs, separated
⅔ cup sugar
¼ cup Mr. Boston Triple
  Sec
¼ cup Amaretto di
  Saronno
¼ teaspoon salt
½ cup finely chopped
  almonds

Beat together egg yolks and sugar until smooth. Cook over low heat, stirring constantly, about 20 minutes or until thickened. Remove from heat and blend in liqueurs. Beat egg whites with salt until stiff, but not dry, peaks form. Blend 1 cup whites into warm yolk mixture. Fold lightened mixture and nuts into remaining whites. Pour into buttered and sugared 2-quart soufflé dish. Bake in preheated 400°F. oven 15–20 minutes. Serve immediately.

6 servings

BRAZILIAN MOCHA PUDDING

Set small rack in bottom of Dutch oven in 3 inches of water. Bring water to boil; reduce heat and keep at a simmer. Beat together shortening and sugar until light and fluffy. Add eggs 1 at a time, beating well after each addition. Blend in nuts and chocolate. Stir together flour, baking powder, salt, and baking soda. Combine milk and brandy. Blend flour mixture alternately with milk mixture into creamed mixture, beginning and ending with flour. Turn into generously greased 1½-quart fluted mold. Cover tightly with aluminum foil. Place on rack in Dutch oven; cover and steam 1 hour and 45 minutes, or until cake tester inserted in center comes out clean. (If necessary, add more boiling water.) Remove mold and cool 15–20 minutes before unmolding. Carefully loosen edges; unmold. Serve warm with Brandy Sauce.

10–12 servings

½ cup shortening
1 cup sugar
2 eggs
1 cup chopped Brazil nuts
1 square (1 ounce) unsweetened chocolate, melted
2 cups flour
1 teaspoon baking powder
1 teaspoon salt
½ teaspoon baking soda
½ cup milk
3 tablespoons Mr. Boston Coffee Flavored Brandy
Brandy Sauce (see below)

Brandy Sauce

Combine milk, sugar, cornstarch, and salt. Cook over low heat until slightly thickened. Stir in beaten eggs; continue cooking until thickened. Remove from heat. Stir in brandy. Serve sauce with pudding.

1½ cups milk
¼ cup sugar
1 tablespoon cornstarch
⅛ teaspoon salt
2 eggs, beaten
2 tablespoons Mr. Boston Five Star Brandy

TRADITIONAL STRAWBERRY SHORTCAKE

2 cups flour
4 tablespoons sugar
1 tablespoon baking
  powder
1 teaspoon salt
½ cup butter or
  shortening
½–¾ cup half-and-half or
  milk
1 quart strawberries,
  sliced
2 tablespoons Mr.
  Boston Triple Sec
Orange Whipped Cream
  (see below)

Stir together flour, 2 tablespoons sugar, baking powder, and salt. Cut in butter until mixture resembles coarse crumbs. Blend in enough half-and-half to make a soft dough. Knead gently on lightly floured surface, 30 seconds. Roll out to ½-inch thickness. Cut out shortcakes with floured 2-inch biscuit cutter and place on ungreased baking sheet. Bake in preheated 450°F. oven 10–12 minutes or until lightly browned. Split warm biscuits. Combine strawberries, Triple Sec, and remaining 2 tablespoons sugar; stir to blend. Spoon over biscuit bottoms, top with remaining biscuit halves, and spoon strawberries over top. Top with Orange Whipped Cream.

12 servings

Orange Whipped Cream

1 cup heavy cream
2 tablespoons Mr.
  Boston Triple Sec
1 tablespoon sugar
½ teaspoon grated
  orange peel
⅛ teaspoon nutmeg

Whip all ingredients together until stiff.

ITALIAN LOVE CAKE

Cut cake into 3 layers. Sprinkle each layer with 2 tablespoons Amaretto di Saronno. Spread layer of pistachio ice cream on bottom cake layer. Top with second cake layer and a layer of strawberry ice cream. Top with third cake layer. Beat cream with remaining 2 tablespoons Amaretto di Saronno until stiff peaks form. Frost cake with whipped cream and freeze. Spread melted chocolate in ¼-inch layer on foil; chill until chocolate hardens. Cut chocolate into small hearts with cookie cutter and arrange on top of cake. Keep cake frozen until ready to serve.

one 9-inch round cake

1 angel food cake
½ cup Amaretto di Saronno
1 pint pistachio ice cream, softened
1 pint strawberry ice cream, softened
2 cups heavy cream
1 six-ounce package semi-sweet chocolate chips, melted

COFFEE BRANDIED CAKE

Beat together butter and sugars until light and fluffy. Add eggs and beat at high speed for 3 minutes. Stir together dry ingredients. Combine milk and brandy. Add flour mixture alternately with liquid to creamed mixture, beginning and ending with flour. Pour into greased 9×13-inch pan. Bake in preheated 350°F. oven 35–40 minutes or until cake springs back when lightly touched. Serve warm or cold with Cinnamon Cream and cherries.

one 9×13-inch cake

¾ cup butter, softened
1 cup sugar
½ cup light brown sugar
3 eggs
2 cups flour
1 tablespoon cocoa
2 teaspoons baking powder
1 teaspoon salt
1 teaspoon soda
½ cup milk
½ cup Mr. Boston Coffee Flavored Brandy
Cinnamon Cream (see below)
15 Maraschino cherries

111

Cinnamon Cream

1 cup heavy cream
2 tablespoons sugar
1 teaspoon cinnamon
1 tablespoon Mr. Boston
  Coffee Flavored
  Brandy

Whip cream until frothy. Gradually beat in sugar, cinnamon, and brandy; continue beating until stiff peaks form.

MOCHA ROLL

4 eggs, separated
½ cup sugar
1 cup flour
½ teaspoon baking
  powder
½ teaspoon salt
½ teaspoon nutmeg
Confectioners' sugar
Chocolate Frosting (see
  below)
Coffee Filling (see below)

Beat egg yolks until thick and lemon-colored; add ¼ cup sugar and beat until very thick. Beat egg whites until foamy; gradually add remaining ¼ cup sugar and beat until stiff, but not dry, peaks form. Fold egg yolk mixture into egg whites. Stir together flour, baking powder, salt, and nutmeg. Gently fold into egg mixture, a third at a time. Pour into 10½ × 15½-inch jelly roll pan that has been greased and lined with wax paper. Bake in preheated 350°F. oven 15–18 minutes or until lightly browned. Remove from pan immediately. Place on towel that has been generously dusted with confectioners' sugar. Roll up cake jelly-roll fashion starting with narrow end; cool. Unroll, fill with Coffee Filling, reroll, and frost with Chocolate Frosting.

10–12 servings

Coffee Filling

Sprinkle gelatin over water; let stand 5 minutes. Heat, stirring constantly, until gelatin dissolves and mixture comes to a boil. Remove from heat and cool to room temperature. Beat cream until stiff peaks form. Add sugar, liqueur, and gelatin; blend thoroughly and chill until mixture mounds.

1 tablespoon unflavored gelatin
2 tablespoons cold water
2 cups heavy cream
3 tablespoons confectioners' sugar
3 tablespoons Expresso Coffee Liqueur

Chocolate Frosting

Melt butter and chocolate over low heat or in double boiler. Add sugar, salt, crème de cacao, and 2 tablespoons milk. Beat until smooth. Add enough additional milk to reach desired spreading consistency.

3 tablespoons butter
2 squares (2 ounces) unsweetened chocolate
3 cups confectioners' sugar
¼ teaspoon salt
2 tablespoons Mr. Boston Crème de Cacao
5–6 tablespoons milk

GÂTEAU DE CASSIS

8 eggs whites
½ cup sugar
1 cup butter
1½ cups sugar
3½ cups self-rising flour
1 cup milk
1 tablespoon Mr. Boston Crème de Cassis
Cassis Filling (see below)
Whipped Cream Frosting (see below)

Beat egg whites until foamy. Gradually add ½ cup sugar, beating until stiff, but not dry, peaks form; set aside. Beat together butter and 1½ cups sugar until light and fluffy. Add flour alternately with milk to creamed mixture, beginning and ending with flour; beat well after each addition. Fold in beaten egg whites and crème de cassis. Turn into four 8-inch round pans that have been greased and lined with wax paper. Bake in preheated 350°F. oven 20–25 minutes or until done. Cool 10 minutes before removing from pans. Cool completely. Spread cooled Cassis Filling between layers. Spread Whipped Cream Frosting over top and sides.

four 8-inch round layers

Cassis Filling

¼ cup butter
1½ cups sugar
8 egg yolks, lightly beaten
½ cup Mr. Boston Crème de Cassis
½ cup golden raisins
½ cup chopped almonds

Melt butter in saucepan or double boiler; stir in sugar, egg yolks, crème de cassis, and raisins. Cook over low heat or in double boiler until very thick, 20–25 minutes, stirring frequently. Remove from heat, cool, and stir in nuts.

Whipped Cream Frosting

1 cup whipping cream
¼ cup powdered sugar
3 tablespoons Mr. Boston Crème de Cassis

Beat cream until stiff peaks form. Add sugar and crème de cassis and beat until thoroughly blended.

114

RASPBERRY MOUSSE MERINGUE PIE

Beat together egg whites and salt until foamy. Gradually beat in sugar until stiff, but not dry, peaks form. Spread ⅔ of the mixture evenly over the bottom and sides of a greased 10-inch-deep-dish pie pan. Place remaining meringue in pastry bag fitted with a star tip. Press rosettes of meringue onto outer edge of pie pan. Sprinkle shell with sliced almonds. Bake in preheated 275°F. oven 40–45 minutes or until lightly browned and hard to the touch. Turn off oven and let shell cool in oven. Press raspberry purée through sieve to remove seeds. Stir gelatin into purée and cook over low heat until gelatin is dissolved, stirring constantly. Stir in Amaretto di Saronno. Chill until syrupy. Fold in whipped cream. Chill until mixture mounds. Spoon into pie shell and garnish with raspberries. Chill until firm, 2–3 hours.

one 10-inch pie

4 egg whites, at room temperature
¼ teaspoon salt
1 cup sugar
⅓ cup sliced almonds
2 ten-ounce packages frozen raspberries, thawed and puréed
1 tablespoon unflavored gelatin
¼ cup Amaretto di Saronno
2 cups heavy cream, whipped
Fresh raspberries or additional thawed and drained frozen raspberries

CHOCO-MINT CREAM PUFFS

1 cup water
½ cup butter
1 cup flour
⅛ teaspoon salt
4 eggs
Crème de Cacao Filling
    (see below)
Choco-Mint Frosting (see
    below)

Bring water and butter to boil, stirring until butter melts. Add flour and salt all at once. Reduce heat. Cook, stirring vigorously, until mixture is smooth and forms a soft ball, 1–2 minutes. Cool slightly. Add eggs one at a time, beating well after each. Drop by well-rounded tablespoonfuls onto greased baking sheet. Bake in preheated 400°F. oven 30–40 minutes or until firm. Cool completely. Cut off top; fill with chilled Crème de Cacao Filling. Replace top and frost with Choco-Mint Frosting.

12 puffs

Crème de Cacao Filling

6 eggs, beaten
½ cup sugar
3 cups half-and-half,
    scalded
¼ cup Mr. Boston Crème
    de Cacao

Combine eggs and sugar; add scalded half-and-half ½ cup at a time, beating well after each addition. Cook over medium heat, stirring constantly, until mixture thickens. Remove from heat; stir in crème de cacao. Cool to room temperature and chill.

Choco-Mint Frosting

Melt chocolate chips in half-and-half, stirring occasionally. Stir in liqueurs. If necessary, beat until smooth. Add more half-and-half, if needed, to attain spreading consistency. Cool.

1 twelve-ounce package semi-sweet chocolate chips
2–3 tablespoons half-and-half
3 tablespoons Mr. Boston Crème de Cacao
1½ tablespoons Mr. Boston Crème de Menthe (white)

CARROT TORTE

Beat together egg yolks, ½ cup sugar, and ¼ cup Mandarine Napoleon until thick and lemon-colored, 4–5 minutes. Fold in carrots, walnuts, raisins, bread crumbs, and cinnamon. Beat egg whites until foamy, gradually add remaining ¼ cup sugar, and beat until stiff, but not dry, peaks form. Fold egg whites into egg yolk mixture; blend thoroughly. Place in three 8-inch round pans that have been greased and lined with wax paper. Bake in preheated 350°F. oven 25–30 minutes or until cake springs back when lightly pressed. Cool slightly, remove from pans, and cool completely. Blend cream cheese, remaining 2 tablespoons Mandarine Napoleon, and enough milk to attain spreading consistency. Spread cream cheese mixture between layers and on top of cake.

three 8-inch round layers

6 eggs, separated
¾ cup sugar
6 tablespoons Mandarine Napoleon
1 cup finely grated carrots
1 cup ground walnuts
⅔ cup light raisins
¼ cup fine, dry bread crumbs
½ teaspoon cinnamon
2 eight-ounce packages cream cheese
¼–⅓ cup milk

NAPOLEON TORTE

6 eggs, separated
6 tablespoons
    Mandarine Napoleon
1½ cups sugar
1½ cups fine, dry bread
    crumbs
1 cup ground almonds
1 tablespoon baking
    powder
Napoleon Butter Cream
    (see below)

Beat together egg yolks and Mandarine Napoleon until frothy. Add 1 cup sugar and beat until thick and lemon-colored, about 5 minutes. Stir together bread crumbs, nuts, and baking powder; blend into egg yolk mixture. Beat egg whites until foamy; gradually add remaining ½ cup sugar, beating until stiff, but not dry, peaks form. Fold egg whites into batter. Pour into three 8-inch round pans that have been greased and lined with wax paper. Bake in preheated 350°F. oven 30–35 minutes, or until cake springs back when lightly pressed. Cool cake 15 minutes in pans; remove. Cool completely, then split each layer in half. Spread about ½ cup Napoleon Butter Cream between each layer and on top. Store in refrigerator until serving.

two 8-inch round layers

Napoleon Butter Cream

1 cup milk
¼ cup flour
1 cup butter, softened
1 cup sugar
2 tablespoons
    Mandarine Napoleon

Blend milk and flour until smooth; cook over medium-low heat until thickened, stirring constantly. Cool to room temperature. Beat together butter and sugar until light and fluffy. Beat in Mandarine Napoleon. Gradually beat in cooled flour mixture. If too thin to spread, chill until thickened.

CHOCOLATE RUM TART

Sprinkle gelatin over water; let stand 5 minutes. Heat, stirring constantly, until gelatin is dissolved and mixture comes to a boil. Cool to room temperature. Beat egg yolks and ½ cup sugar until thick and lemon-colored. Add gelatin and chocolate; blend well. Beat egg whites until foamy, gradually beat in remaining sugar, and continue beating until stiff, but not dry, peaks form. Fold egg whites, then whipped cream and rum into chocolate mixture. Spoon into pie shell and chill 3–4 hours.

one 9-inch pie

1 tablespoon unflavored gelatin
¼ cup cold water
3 eggs, separated
¾ cup sugar
2 two-ounce squares unsweetened chocolate, melted
1 cup whipping cream, whipped
¼ cup Mr. Boston Virgin Islands Dark Rum
Baked 9-inch pie shell

FRESH PEACH TART

Stir together flour, nuts, and salt. Cut in butter until mixture resembles coarse crumbs. Blend in water, 1–2 tablespoons at a time, until mixture forms ball. Roll out dough on lightly floured surface to a 14-inch circle. Center on 12-inch tart or pizza pan. Flute edges; prick crust with fork and bake in preheated 400°F. oven 5–8 minutes. Cool 5–10 minutes. Purée 2 peaches with 2 tablespoons Amaretto di Saronno and nutmeg. Spread mixture over bottom of pastry. Thinly slice remaining peaches and arrange in circular pattern over pastry. Drizzle with 2 tablespoons Amaretto di Saronno. Bake in preheated 400°F. oven 5–8 minutes. Combine peach preserves and remaining 1 tablespoon Amaretto di Saronno; spread over warm tart. Cool before serving.

One 12-inch round tart

1½ cups flour
½ cup ground almonds
½ teaspoon salt
½ cup butter
½–⅔ cup cold water
6 fresh peaches, pitted and peeled
5 tablespoons Amaretto di Saronno
⅛ teaspoon nutmeg
¼ cup peach preserves

BAKLAVA

1 cup butter, melted
¼ cup oil
½ pound filo dough
1½ cups finely chopped
　walnuts
1½ cups finely chopped
　almonds
1½ cups sugar
½ cup Mr. Boston Five
　Star Brandy
½ cup water
2 tablespoons honey
2 tablespoons lemon
　juice

Blend butter and oil. Brush over bottom and sides of 9 × 13-inch baking pan. Place layer of filo dough on bottom. Brush with butter mixture. Stir together nuts and sprinkle ¼ cup over pastry. Cover with another layer of pastry, brush with butter, and sprinkle with ¼ cup nuts. Repeat procedure ending with pastry layer. Score pastry to form diamond shapes. Bake in pre- heated 350°F. oven 30 minutes. Reduce heat to 300°F. and bake until pastry is browned, about 30 minutes more. Combine remaining ingredients in saucepan; bring to a boil and boil 5 minutes. Remove from heat. Pour over baked Baklava and let stand at least 10 minutes before serving.

10 to 12 servings

CREAMY GIN SOUR

Place all ingredients in blender jar; blend at high speed 30 seconds or until frothy. Serve in wine glasses.

4–6 servings

½ cup Mr. Boston English Market Gin
½ cup lime juice
½ cup lemon juice
½ cup heavy cream
¼ cup Mr. Boston Triple Sec
1 tablespoon sugar
¾ cup crushed ice
10 ounces club soda

PINEAPPLE COOLER

Place all ingredients in blender jar; blend at high speed until frothy.

Serve in Collins glasses.

4 servings

*Any citrus juice and sherbet can be substituted.

2 cups pineapple juice*
¾ cup Mr. Boston Anisette
1 cup pineapple sherbet*

CITRUS FROST

Place all ingredients in blender jar; blend at high speed until frothy.

Serve in tall stemmed glasses. Garnish with lemon twist.

4–6 servings

1 quart lemon sherbet
1 cup Mandarine Napoleon
10 ounces club soda
Lemon twists

STRAWBERRIES IN CREAM

2 cups vanilla ice cream
2 cups frozen or fresh
   strawberries
1 cup Mr. Boston White
   Crème de Cacao
Whole strawberries

Place all ingredients in blender jar; blend at high speed until smooth.

Serve in champagne glasses. Garnish with whole strawberries.

4–6 servings

CITRUS BANANA FLIP

1 ripe banana, cut in
   pieces
10 ounces club soda
⅔ cup orange juice
   concentrate
⅔ cup milk
½ cup Mr. Boston Virgin
   Islands Dark Rum
½ cup lime juice
3 tablespoons brown
   sugar
½ cup crushed ice

Place all ingredients in blender jar; blend at high speed 30 seconds or

until smooth. Serve in Collins glasses.

4–6 servings

FRUITY SMASH

1 pint vanilla ice cream
⅓ cup Mr. Boston Cherry
   Flavored Brandy
⅓ cup Mr. Boston Crème
   de Banana
Maraschino cherries

Place all ingredients in blender jar; blend at high speed until smooth.

Serve in champagne glasses. Garnish with cherries.

4–6 servings

Fresh Peach Tart

Drinks

PINEAPPLE BANANA REFRESHER

Place all ingredients in blender jar; blend at high speed until smooth. Serve in high ball glasses. Garnish with pineapple wedge and banana slice on toothpick.

4–5 servings

2 cups pineapple juice
1 cup pineapple sherbet
½ cup Mr. Boston Crème de Banana
½ cup Mr. Boston Virgin Islands Dark Rum
Pineapple wedges
Banana slices

PEACHY AMARETTO

Place all ingredients in blender jar; blend at high speed 30 seconds or until smooth. Serve in tall stemmed glasses.

3–4 servings

1 cup vanilla ice cream
1 cup peaches
1 cup Amaretto di Saronno

STRAWBERRY BANANA SPRITZ

Place all ingredients in blender jar; blend at high speed 30 seconds or until smooth. Serve in tall stemmed glasses. Garnish with whole strawberries.

4–6 servings

1 pint vanilla ice cream
1 cup fresh or frozen strawberries
1 cup Mr. Boston Crème de Banana
10 ounces club soda
Whole strawberries

123

APRICOT CREAM SPRITZ

¾ cup milk
½ cup apricot nectar
¼ cup crushed ice
2 tablespoons Mr.
Boston Apricot
Flavored Brandy
2 cups Torre dei Conti
Asti Spumante

Place milk, apricot nectar, ice, and brandy in blender jar; blend at high speed until smooth. Pour equal amounts into 6 large wine glasses. Add about ⅓ cup wine to each. Stir and serve.

4–6 servings

CAFÉ AU LAIT FRAPPE

2 cups half-and-half
2 cups strong coffee
¼ cup Mr. Boston Coffee
Flavored Brandy
¼ cup Mr. Boston Five
Star Brandy
⅓ cup sugar
½ teaspoon cinnamon

Combine all ingredients and heat to just below boiling. Freeze 3 hours, whisking twice to break up ice crystals. Serve when slushy in tall stemmed glass.

4–6 servings

ICED COFFEE À L'ORANGE

1 quart vanilla ice cream
4 teaspoons instant
coffee
1 cup Mr. Boston Triple
Sec
Orange slices

Place all ingredients in blender jar; blend at high speed until smooth. Serve in tall stemmed glasses. Garnish with orange slices.

5–6 servings

ICY RUMMED CACAO

Place all ingredients in blender jar; blend at high speed until smooth.

Serve in champagne glasses. Garnish with shaved chocolate.

4–6 servings

1 quart vanilla ice cream
½ cup Mr. Boston Virgin Islands Dark Rum
½ cup Mr. Boston Dark Crème de Cacao
Shaved chocolate

CHOCOLATE ALMOND CREAM

Place all ingredients in blender jar; blend until smooth. Serve in tall stemmed glasses. Garnish with shaved chocolate.

4–6 servings

1 quart vanilla ice cream
½ cup Amaretto di Saronno
½ cup Mr. Boston Crème de Cacao
Shaved chocolate

HOT APPLE BRANDY

Simmer all ingredients over low heat 30 minutes. Serve warm in brandy snifters.

6–8 servings

6 cups unsweetened apple juice
1½ cups Mr. Boston Apricot Flavored Brandy
3 cinnamon sticks
½ teaspoon ground cloves

125

Menu Guide

FORMAL DINNER

Chicken Liver Pâté
Anisette Steamed Fish
Cheesey Rice Bake
Orange and Onion Salad
Almond Orange Soufflé

Serve with Lawrence Chardonnay

BUFFET DINNER PARTY

Crab Legs or Shrimp with Cucumber Seafood Dunk (cold)
Seafruit Stuffed Mushrooms
Senegalese Soup
Orange Brandied Leg of Lamb
Orange Rye Bread
Broccoli Timbales
Vegetable Medley
Sliced Tomatoes with Bleu Cheese Dressing
Baked Pears with Ginger Caramel
Choco-Mint Cream Puffs

Serve with Lawrence Cabernet Savignon

HOLIDAY DINNER

Broiled Stuffed Oysters
Prime Rib Roast with Yorkshire Pudding and Scotch Gravy
Roasted Potatoes
Glazed Baby Carrots
Horseradish Cream
Choice of Tossed Green Salad or Endive with Vinaigrette
Strawberries in Almond Cream

Serve with Fine Chilled Imported Champagne
Finish with Espresso

COCKTAIL PARTY

Seafood Toast (hot)
Seafruit Stuffed Mushrooms (cold)
Tipsy Cheese Spread (cold)
Veal-Stuffed Apples (hot)
Broiled Chicken Drummettes (hot)
Sweet and Sour Sausage Balls (hot)
Vegetable Terrine (cold)
Mushrooms à la Grecque (cold)

ETHNIC DINNERS

GREEK

Potage of Artichoke
Chilled Stuffed Mussels
Braised Lamb Shanks au Vin Rouge
Plain Pasta or Rice
Pita Bread
Baklava

Serve with Lawrence Rosé

ORIENTAL

Spicy Baby Back Ribs
Swordfish Teriyaki with Plain Rice
Gingered Green Beans and Peppers
Salad of Pea Pods, Chinese Cabbage,
Radishes, Mushrooms, Bean Sprouts,
and Fresh Broccoli, served with:
Oriental Salad Dressing
Frosted Oranges Saronno

Begin with hot sake
Finish with tea

GERMAN

Tipsy Cheese Spread
Pumpernickel Bread
Bavarian Apple Pot Roast
Almond-Poppy Seed Noodles
Green Salad with Vinaigrette
Mocha Chip Mousse

Serve with icy cold beer

ITALIAN

Cognac Steamed Mussels
Veal Scallopini Rolls
Fusilli with Whiskey Cream Sauce
Caesar Salad
Italian Love Cake

Serve with Lawrence Fumé Blanc

SIT DOWN BRUNCH

Apricot Cream Spritz
Papaya Pineapple Compote
Shrimp and Eggs Royale
Tomato Wedges on Bed of Lettuce
Coffee Brandied Cake

BUFFET BRUNCH

Asti Fruit Bowl (cold)
Olive Cheese Bread (room temperature)
Brandy Bacon Biscuits (room temperature)
Asparagus Prosciutto Bake (hot)
Salmon-Stuffed Tomatoes (hot)
Sherried Eggs in Potato Skins (hot)
Mexican Egg Pie (hot)
Curried Avocado Salad (cold)
Fresh Peach Tart (room temperature)
Mocha Pots de Crème (cold)

Serve with Fine Chilled Imported Champagne

LIQUOR INDEX

BRANDY

Mr. Boston Five Star Brandy
Baklava, 120
Frosty Fruit Nectar, 19
Brandied Onion Soup, 19
South Seas Fish Sauté, 28
Venetian Stew, 32
Cornish Hens with Apple-Grape Stuffing, 37
Veal- and Ham-Stuffed Turkey, 39
Veal with Dijon Mustard Sauce, 50
Anchovy-Stuffed Veal Chops, 51
Bavarian Apple Pot Roast, 42
Brandy Bacon Biscuits, 100
Pork Sausage Hash with Poached Eggs, 84
Creamy Bleu Cheese Dressing, 80
Café au Lait Frappe, 124
Brandy Sauce, 109

Mr. Boston Apricot Flavored Brandy
Hot Apple Brandy, 125
Apricot Brandy Sauce, 64
Chutney Dressing, 79
Apricot Cream Spritz, 124
Frosty Fruit Nectar, 19
All-Purpose Fish Poaching Liquor, 34
Duck with Apricots, 40
Tangy Turkey Breast, 38
Fruit-Stuffed Pork Loin with Apricot Glaze, 55
Apricot Orange Butter, 48
Swiss Wheat Bread, 101
Rotini with Apricot Brandy Sauce, 64

Mr. Boston Coffee Flavored Brandy
Lamb Rib chops with Coffee Brandy Cream Sauce, 54
Coffee Brandied Cake with Cinnamon Cream, 111
Mocha Chip Mousse, 107
Brazilian Mocha Pudding, 109
Café au Lait Frappe, 124
Mocha Pots de Crème, 108

Mr. Boston Ginger Flavored Brandy
Baked Pears with Ginger Caramel, 107
Sweet and Sour Sausage Balls, 11

Teriyaki-Marinated Swordfish, 25
Ginger-Limed Pike, 30
Ginger Cream Chicken, 36
London Broil Oriental, 46
Gingered Green Beans and Peppers, 61
Oriental Dressing, 78
Oriental Shrimp with Ginger Dipping Sauce, 29

Mr. Boston Peach Flavored Brandy
Peaches and Creamed Veal, 50
Flank Steak Supreme, 43
Peachy French Toast with Sausage, 89
Fanciful Fruit Salad, 73

Mr. Boston Cherry Flavored Brandy
Cheese Fondue, 15
Roquefort-Stuffed Pears, 14
Cornish Hens with Bing Cherry Sauce, 38
Plummed Chicken, 35
Fruity Smash, 122

Rémy Martin V.S.O.P. Cognac
Mocha Pots de Crème, 108
Cognac Steamed Mussels, 5
Roquefort-Stuffed Pears, 14
Sole Lunay, 25
Duck with Orange Prune Sauce, 41
Anisette Chicken, 35
Sirloin Patties Elegante, 43
Horseradish Cream, 47
Salmon-Stuffed Tomatoes, 91
Tomato Salad with Cognac Cream Dressing, 78
Seafood with Vegetables and Whiskey, 33

MR. BOSTON CORDIALS

Crème de Menthe (white)
Mint Fried Chicken, 36
Sweet and Sour Lamb, 54
Choco-Mint Cream Puffs, 116

Crème de Cacao
Choco-Mint Cream Puffs, 116
Strawberries in Cream, 122

Expresso Coffee Liqueur
Mocha Roll, 112

LIQUORS

**Gin: Mr. Boston English Market Gin
or Glenmore Gin**
Sunny Scallop Surprise, 8
Marinated Brussel Sprouts, 74
Devonshire Potato Salad, 76
Tipsy Cheese Spread, 16
Creamy Ratatouille Soup, 22
Veal Kidneys with Gin, 53
Fried Pork and Cabbage, 57
A Dilly of a Butter, 49
Olive Cheese Bread, 102
Red Cabbage Sauté with Gin, 68
Cucumber Salad, 74
Creamy Gin Sour, 121

Vodka: Mr. Boston or Glenmore Vodka
Cucumber Seafood Dunk, 8
Imperial Borscht, 17
Bloody Mary Muffins, 100
Caesar Salad, 75
Caviar Dressing, 80
Fried Pork and Cabbage, 57

Tequila: Gavilan or Gavilan Especial Tequila
Mexican Egg Pie, 86
Crab and Grapefruit Salad, 91

Rum: Mr. Boston Virgin Islands Rum
Light
    Italian Sweet Bread, 90
    Pineapple Banana Refresher, 123
Dark
    Rice Cakes, 90
    Chocolate Rum Tart, 119
    Rum Raisin Baked Apples, 105
    Citrus Banana Flip, 122
    Icy Rummed Cocoa, 125

WHISKEYS
Bourbons: Yellowstone Mellow Mash,
Yellowstone Straight Bourbon Whiskey,
Old Kentucky Tavern Straight Bourbon
Whiskey, and Old Thompson American Whiskey
Lemon Garlic butter, 48
Potato-Apple Casserole, 63
Pumpernickel Bread, 96
Corn and Okra Fritters, 69
Horseradish Steak Sauce, 47
Whiskey-Sauced Fish, 31
Fusilli with Whiskey Cream Sauce, 65

Scotch: Desmond & Duff Deluxe Scotch
Swordfish Skewers, 27
Curried Shrimp Balls with Coconut Cream, 27
Veal Scallopini Rolls, 49
Cranberry-Glazed Ribs, 56
Yorkshire Pudding, 44
Scotch Gravy, 45
Savory Scotch Butter, 48
Seafood with Vegetables and Whiskey, 33

WINES
Balfour Cream Sherry
Seafood Stuffed Mushrooms, 7
Vegetable Terrine, 12
Fish Bites with Cream Sherry Sauce, 10
Sherried Fish Chowder, 20
Potage of Artichoke, 18
Pork Tenderloin with Cream, 56
Sherried Eggs in Potato Skins, 85
Eggs Florentine, 83
Asparagus Proscuitini Bake, 88
Shrimp and Eggs Royale, 90
Vegetable Medley, 62
Cheesey Rice Bake, 66
Wild Sherry Rice, 67
Mushroom Cream Sherry Sauté, 69

Torre dei Conti Asti Spumante
Chicken in Champagne Sauce, 34
Asti Fruit Bowl, 84
Apricot Cream Spritz, 124

RECIPE INDEX